Pastor Helen

ECLIPSE
of the
HEART

By Helen Canty

ZOË LIFE
PUBLISHING
WORDS TO LIVE BY

Published by:
Zoë Life Publishing
P.O. Box 871066
Canton, MI 48187 USA
www.zoelifepub.com

Take note that the name satan and associated names are not capitalized. We choose not to give him any preeminence, even to the point of violating grammatical rules. Throughout Scripture, emphasis is often added by the author.

Author: Helen Canty
Cover Design: Chamira Jones
Editorial Team: Robert Mctyre, Jessica Colvin, and Kumari Ellison

First U.S. Edition 2007

Library of Congress Cataloging-in-Publication Data

Canty, Helen.
  Eclipse of the heart / by Helen Canty. -- 1st U.S. ed.
      p. cm.
  Includes bibliographical references and index.
  ISBN-13: 978-1-934363-21-8 (hardcover : alk. paper)
  ISBN-10: 1-934363-21-9 (hardcover : alk. paper)
1. Christian life. 2. Christianity--Psychology. 3. Emotions--Religious
aspects--Christianity. I. Title.
BV4501.3.C3655 2007
248.4--dc22
                        2007033373

Summary: The redemptive grace of Christ cannot accomplish its full work when our hearts are crusted over by sin, unforgiveness and bitterness. We allow our sins and secrets to block us. This book instructs how to "uncover our hearts so that the Holy Spirit can have full access to our souls (mind, will and emotions)."

10 Digit ISBN 1-934363-21-9 Hardcover
13 Digit ISBN 978-1-934363-21-8 Hardcover

    1. Religious, Christian, Christian Living, Christian Growth, Adult

For current information about releases by Helen Canty or other releases from
Zoë Life Publishing, visit our web site: http://www.zoelifepub.com

                    Printed in the United States of America

                          # v8 01-14-08

Dedication

To my husband who continuously encouraged me in every aspect, and who never once complained if we ordered carryout for lunch and dinner. Thank you for your kindness and many words of wisdom during an important time in my life.

To my family, especially my children that heard me talk about writing and publishing books for years and never once spoke a discouraging word. You are my legacy.

Finally, to all those at Way of Life who observed me through this whole process and spoke encouraging words—at just the right time!

ECLIPSE
of the
HEART

By Helen Canty

Contents

CONTENTS

1

The Eclipsed Heart

What is man that You are mindful of him, and the son of man that You visit him? For You have made him a little lower than the angels (Elohim, God), and You have crowned him with glory and honor (Psalm 8:4-5).

The contexts of these wonderful scriptures speak about Jesus the Christ, and they also speak to the Glory of the Lord in Creation.

God created man and fashioned him in His own image and in this manner revealed His Glory. He formed man exactly as He desired—spirit, soul and body. Thus in His forming man, God shaped man and placed inside of him a heart fully persuaded toward his Creator. This meant that the thoughts of man's heart were only good and he knew no evil.

Then came the fall of man and his heart became so wicked and evil that Genesis 6:5-7 tells us:

Then the Lord saw that the wickedness of man was great in the earth, and that every intent of the thoughts of his heart was only evil continually. And the Lord was sorry that He had made man on the earth, and He was grieved in His heart. So the Lord said, "I will destroy man, whom I have created, from the face of the earth, both man and beast, creeping thing and birds of the air, for I am sorry that I have made them."

The heart of man was so important to God that He was willing to destroy man because of the wickedness in man's heart. The scriptures show us, however, that not all men had this wickedness; and this became our saving grace.

When we read further, Genesis 6:8 tells us "But Noah found grace in the eyes of the Lord." Thank God for favor, but it was not favor alone that saved man from being wiped off the face of the earth; it was Noah's walk with God. Genesis 6:9b says, "Noah walked with God," which means Noah had a heart of integrity and was blameless before God. This is what Christ has given to us in the new birth experience; a heart of integrity, and we too can walk blameless because of God's grace.

Ezekiel 11:19-20 says:

"Then I will give them one heart, and I will put a new spirit within them (you), and take the stony heart out of their flesh, and give them a heart of flesh. This is the new birth experience which happens when we "confess with our mouth the Lord Jesus and believe in our heart that God has raised Him from the dead, you will be saved" (Romans 10:9).

Jesus, coming to earth as a man, paid the price and removed the stony heart that was keeping man from loving and communicating with his Maker. Our hearts are now restored to the one who created us, "The Almighty God," Maker of Heaven and Earth.

What exactly is this heart that God has changed? Thayer's Greek Lexicon, by Joseph Thayer, defines the word heart (kardia) as the seat and center of all physical and spiritual life, the vigor and sense of physical life, and the center and seat of spiritual life, the soul or mind, as it is the fountain and seat of the thoughts, passions, desires, appetites, affections, purposes, and endeavors.

This may seem like a very technical definition; so to simplify it, we can say the heart is where everything originates in man. Every thought, every decision, every action, regardless if it is good, bad or indifferent, it all comes from the heart.

Isaiah 53:10-11 gives us clarity as to what Jesus did in the heart of man.

Yet it pleased the Lord to bruise (crush) Him; He has put Him to grief. When You make His soul an offering for sin, He shall see His seed, and He shall prolong His days, And the pleasure of the Lord shall prosper in His hand.

The next verse says:

He shall see the labor of His soul, and be satisfied. By His knowledge My righteous Servant shall justify many, For He shall bear their iniquities.

When Christ took away our iniquities on the Cross, it was the stony heart that He took away—the heart that was continually evil as spoken of in Genesis 6:5. Christ's death, burial and resurrection restored our relationship to God; therefore, giving God the legal right to declare us righteous. We are now justified (declared righteous) by faith through the saving grace of Jesus Christ.

Our hearts have been made new; unfortunately, we tend to live our lives through our souls (mind, will and emotions). By this, I mean we allow the issues of life, and the residue from those issues, to dictate who we are in Christ. Doing so induces us to focus on those issues causing us not to function from the newly restored heart; the heart of flesh that Ezekiel 11:19 speaks about. The Lord has clearly said He has taken away the weighted down heart that has been built up over a lifetime; and He has caused it to cease, to disappear. Now it is up to us to allow the heart of flesh to operate in the manner God intended. Let us look at this further.

When Adam was created, he was created perfect. There was no sin in him. He was created to commune with God forever. He was never to experience spiritual or physical death.

Genesis 1:26 says:

Let Us make man in Our image, according to Our likeness, let them have dominion over the fish of the sea, over the birds of the air and over the cattle, over all the earth and over every creeping thing that creeps on the earth.

The awesome part about what God did when He created man was He "breathed into his nostrils the breath of life; and man became a living being" (Genesis 2:7b). God breathed the very essence of Himself into man. Nowhere in scripture can you find where God breathed into the creatures or the animals He created. Nor does scripture say that God made animals in His image; however, it does say that He made man in His image.

Genesis 1:21 tells us that:

God created great sea creatures and every living thing that moves, with which the waters abounded, according to their kind, and every winged bird according to its kind. And God saw that it was good.

With just one breath, God now resides in man's heart. Man now has God's glory-manifesting perfection in his spirit, soul and body, giving him the ability to function just like his God. Adam knew no sickness, no disease, no lack or any other negative emotion. The joy of the Lord was Adam's strength.

In order for us to have what Adam had from the beginning, Jesus had to go to the Cross of Redemption. His dying and resurrection restored us back to the original state that God intended from the beginning. It is because of Jesus that we can now live a victorious life, which is what God intended when He first breathed life into Adam.

God said I "will put a new heart in you and take away the stony heart and give you a heart of flesh. In this heart of flesh is new life."

John 10:10b says, "I have come that they may have life, and

that they may have it more abundantly." The Greek word for this type of life is *Zoë*—a life full of vitality. We now have a life that never gives up, a life that flows with zeal and vigor from deep within the heart, a life that is not only eternal, but a life that has God's continuous blessing.

Jesus paid the price to restore *Zoë* to us through His death, burial, and resurrection. Therefore, when we receive Christ as our Savior and Lord, we are brought back to our original state; the original plan that God intended from the very beginning in the Garden of Eden.

Let me explain it this way. Have you ever gone to the store to purchase an item only to find the item out of stock when you arrived at the store? Upon finding out that what you wanted was out of stock, the salesperson attempted to sell you a different brand that was said to be as good as the original brand. The salesperson tried hard to convince you that there was no difference between the two products; yet all the consumer magazines quoted that the original product that you wanted was the best on the market.

What the salesperson was attempting to do was to sell you a brand that looked to be as good as the original in order to be credited with making the sale. However, you made the wise decision to wait for the original, informing the salesperson that you would return at a later date to make the purchase.

> Satan can only gain access if we allow the issues of life to harden our heart causing the stony heart to be unmovable.

This is Jesus: He paid the price for the original. Now we have "new life" because Christ restored all that was taken, and unjustly retained by satan; therefore, satan can no longer rule in your heart. In fact, "sin has no more dominion over you" (Romans 6:14a).

Satan can only gain access if we allow the issues of life to harden our heart causing the stony heart to be unmovable. This is what the Israelites did.

Psalm 95:8-11 says:

Do not harden your hearts, as in the rebellion, as in the day of trial in the wilderness, when your fathers tested Me; they tried Me, though they saw My work, for forty years I was grieved with that generation, and said, it is a people who go astray in their hearts, and they do not know My ways. So I swore in My wrath, they shall not enter My rest.

A journey that could have been made in eleven days stretched out for a total of forty years. Moses and all those in his generation never set foot in the Promised Land. Because of the hearts of the people, God had to find a whole new generation to do His will.

What Jesus did on the Cross was so profound. Our intellect cannot fathom the depth of Christ's experience on the Cross, nor can we ever duplicate what He did. Since man was responsible for bringing sin into the world, man had to pay the price; therefore, when Jesus came to earth, He was in the form of being fully man and fully God, totally depending on the Holy Spirit to guide Him.

Now we have the ability to be just like our Creator. We now benefit from the second Adam, Jesus, to accomplish all that

God has predestined and purposed for our lives. Had Adam not sinned, we would have lived forever because this was God's plan for man. Think about it for a moment. Why would God create man in His image only for man to die? Yet, God made man just like Himself, a spirit being with a free will. Man was given a will to choose life or death, and man chose death in the Garden.

It took Adam 930 years to physically die because he had to learn how to die. Death was not a part of God's original plan for man. God's original plan was for man to walk in His statutes and keep His laws permanently; but man chose a different plan. Ezekiel 11:20 says that God did this so "that they may walk in My statutes and keep My judgments and do them; and they shall be My people, and I will be their God."

We need to thank God that although man chose a different plan, man's choice did not change the heart of God for man, nor did it change His plan for man. When Jesus died on the Cross, God's statutes and laws were permanently written and binding on the hearts of His people. These permanently binding ordinances will cause us to keep God's judgments and do them.

God's idea of doing His judgments means to work, labor, make, create, instruct, build, accomplish, procure, prepare, earn, offer, sacrifice, and to fulfill. The Word further says that if we do God's commands, He will be our God. The word "be" means to breathe or to come to pass. All that God has breathed into us will come to pass when our heart functions in the manner God designed.

It is important for us to understand how and why the heart finds secret places to hide. The Word says He has taken away the stony heart, the weighted down heart that has been built up over a lifetime, yet we still function out of the stony heart. This is because we have allowed the issues of life to consume our hearts, so much so now the heart God gave fresh and new is hidden and covered.

This is the result of issues in our lives that have burdened the heart into a hidden state. Oftentimes, we are not even aware that we are hiding. We are so consumed with ourselves that our perceptions cause us to blame others for our problems.

God does not want us to hide. When the heart is hidden, we cannot see; therefore, we are not open to honest dialog about ourselves, nor are we open for correction. Also, when the heart is hidden we cannot make sound rational decisions. We tend to make decisions out of frustrations leading to even more problems.

How many times have we called upon the Wisdom of God, only to find that confusion takes over, hindering our decision-making processes? "There is a way that seems right to a man, but its end is the way of death" (Proverbs 16:25).

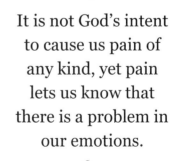

It is not God's intent to cause us pain of any kind, yet pain lets us know that there is a problem in our emotions.

It is the Word of God that can bring healing to those issues we have tucked away in our hearts. We must receive and accept God's Word when uncovering the secret and hidden places of our hearts. Only the Word of God is true, and it is the truth that will set us free.

It is not God's intent to cause us pain of any kind, yet pain lets us know that there is a problem in our emotions that we must allow the Holy Spirit to unearth, and bring our souls (mind, will, emotions) to a place where there is no gap between our spirit and our soul.

One morning while I was praying, the Lord began to show me how the heart looks when it is hidden. The heart becomes covered over like an eclipse. The more issues left to fester in the heart, the more the covering over the heart. There are two types of eclipses—lunar and solar. An eclipse occurs at those times when the moon moves into a position of direct alignment with the Sun and the Earth. The lunar eclipse occurs when the full Moon passes through the shadow of the Earth, and a solar eclipse occurs when the new Moon passes directly between the Sun and the Earth.

In the solar eclipse, the Moon's shadow is swept across the Earth causing daytime to briefly turn into darkness. The eclipse brings about a dulling overshadowing of the correct process, which is for light to be seen, yet darkness has taken over.

There is a cutting off of the light. So it is with our heart when it is hidden. There is a dulling that blocks the correct process of the Son, Jesus, causing darkness to take over, revealing only one side, and cutting off the Light of Christ. In John 8:12 Jesus says, "I am the light of the world. He who follows Me shall not walk in darkness, but have the light of life."

Just like the Earth needs the Sun to survive, so we God's children need the "Son" to survive. Earth needs the Sun's warmth, and so we need the Son of God to warm our hearts, and keep our hearts fully persuaded and focused on Christ.

The heart that is not fully persuaded and focused on Christ is a heart that will become overshadowed cutting off the light to our souls (mind, will and emotions). When an eclipse occurs in the natural sphere, darkness starts to come. The dulling obscures the fame or glory of the Sun. When an eclipse of the heart occurs, the light in the heart is cut off or the glory of Christ, who is actually giving the light, is obscured thus not allowing the light of Christ to shine through the heart to our souls.

Although Jesus took away the stony heart, the weighted down heart that has been built up over a lifetime, when we do not crucify the flesh daily (the operative word here is daily) we set our hearts up to receive from the issues of life instead of the Light of Christ through His Word. We may even suppress the negative issues, and try and function as if the issues do not exist leaving us with a heart deeply covered.

Many things cause our hearts to be covered, but some of the more common things include past and present environments, self-esteem issues, emotions, and lack of embracing Christ as Lord over our lives.

We may not be responsible for the environment we experienced as a child; however, we are responsible for the environment we presently choose. In fact, we should allow the Holy Spirit to choose not only our environment, but I will go as far as to say we should listen to the Holy Spirit in developing friendships.

Over the years, my close friends have been very few because I have learned that it is not necessary or important to be friends with every person I meet. People enter our lives for a season, and when the season is over God moves them on. Therefore, if I allow the Holy Spirit to guide my feelings in choosing friends, those friendships tend to be more fruitful.

Unfortunately, our childhood environment may have been painful setting up wounds in our emotions. These painful emotions now cause us to respond negatively to most circumstances that arise in our life. Although God loves us and is compassionate, He still does not want our emotions ruling and controlling how we live.

He does not hear our complaining nor does He accept our blaming others for our past and present behavior. The most horrid past of any kind has been overcome by the Blood of the Lamb. Out-of-control emotions lead to poor self-esteem and destruction, convincing our hearts we are not worthy to receive what God has for us, and causing our hearts to be covered with negative emotions.

The most horrid past of any kind has been overcome by the Blood of the Lamb.

This leaves us to follow our flesh instead of our spirit which is a major problem because "I know that in me (that is, in my flesh) nothing good dwells" (Romans 7:18a).

Instead of following our flesh, we should seek the Lord first in all that we do. Fortunately, many have accepted Jesus as Savior; but unfortunately, many have neglected to make Him Lord over everything in their lives.

Romans 8:12-16 explains it this way: "Therefore, brethren, we are debtors—not to the flesh, to live according to the flesh. For if you live according to the flesh you will die; but if by the Spirit you put to death the deeds of the body, you will live. For as many as are led by the Spirit of God, these are sons of God. For you did not receive the spirit of bondage again to fear, but you received the Spirit of adoption by whom we cry out, Abba, Father."

This is who we are. We have son-ship through the Spirit of the Living God. We must thoroughly embrace who we are in Christ, and receive Christ as both Savior and Lord over all.

Yes, we are saved; however, we received more than just salvation at Calvary. We received a Father who breathed His very life into us fully knowing that we would make mistakes on this earth, yet He gave us total forgiveness and repentance so that satan could not condemn us.

According to scripture "there is therefore now no condemnation to those who are in Christ Jesus, who do not walk according to the flesh, but according to the Spirit" (Romans 8:1). When we walk in the flesh, we shut off our relationship and communication we have with God. He does not leave us, we leave Him.

Romans 8:38-39 tells us, "For I am persuaded that neither death nor life, nor angels nor principalities nor powers, nor things present nor things to come, nor height nor depth, nor any other created thing, shall be able to separate us from the love of God which is in Christ Jesus our Lord."

We stop studying God's Word, we stop praying as we should, and we stop fellowshipping with other believers unknowingly relinquishing our rightful place in God. Therefore, the separation that arises is fully on our part, not on God's part.

Now the issues of life are in control as to how we communicate or if we communicate with God and others. We no longer look to Him as our source; instead, we overdose on self-pity, self-will, self-views, self-thoughts, and self-opinions; leaving no room for the Word of God in our hearts.

We all have secret places in our hearts that need to be uncovered; and although the process of uncovering these hidden areas of the heart may be painful, the uncovering is not to rehearse the pain, but to bring healing so we can have honest relationships.

The irony of a hidden heart is that God knows our hearts anyway. God, the Creator, has perfect knowledge of who we are. We cannot hide from Him. Psalms 139:12 says, "Indeed, the darkness shall not hide from You. But the night shines as the day. The darkness and the light are both alike to You." We should want the true spirit of any problem revealed, so that the enemy does not cause us to be deceived.

Understand, anytime the truth is hidden, deception comes to cloud our mind. Deception's job is to bring about a lack of trust in our heart, to cause us to begin questioning every decision we make so much so that now we are in bondage in our thought processes. This is not what God wants for our life.

John 8:32 says, "And you shall know the truth, and the truth shall make you free". The freedom that Jesus is speaking about here will help us to truly be a Christian (Christ-like). We can be in a place of letting the Word of God thoroughly rule in our heart instead of a place of bondage.

> Helping others *is* an act of Christianity.

Know that Christianity is not just what we do to help others, helping others *is* an act of Christianity. How can we honestly help others when we do not allow God to change who we are. We should be changing every single day; looking more like Christ.

The real test of this change is in our character. It is what we allow Christ to do in our hearts to bring about change in our character. There are to be no unhealthy roots lingering in our hearts.

I am reminded of a study I did a while ago about the fig tree that Jesus cursed in Mark 11. "Now the next day, when they had come out from Bethany, He was hungry, and seeing from afar a fig tree having leaves, He went to see if perhaps He would find something on it. When He came to it, He found nothing but leaves, for it was not the season for figs. In response Jesus said to it, let no one eat fruit from you ever again, and His disciples heard it" (Mark 11:12-14).

The fig tree looked good to Jesus from a far off, but upon a closer look, the fig tree had nothing to offer. There was no fruit. This is what happens to us when negative emotions consume our hearts and cause us to hide. We look good on the outside, but we have nothing to offer from the inside.

This tree Jesus cursed was doing what it knew to do. It did not even realize that it had a problem. We go through life much in the same manner, doing what we know to do even though our hearts are hidden and full of pain.

Is there some symbolism present as to why Jesus cursed the fig tree? Some theologians believe that the fruit eaten by Adam and Eve was from the fig tree. This is possible as the fig tree is one of the oldest fruit trees known to man. Regardless, we know that Adam and Eve used fig leaves to cover themselves because Genesis 3:7 says, "...and they sewed fig leaves together and made themselves coverings."

If this is the fruit that Adam and Eve ate, Jesus cursed the very fruit man ate in the Garden which aided in the fall of man.

This is one of the questions we can ask when we get to heaven.

Nevertheless, initially I believed there was a problem with the roots of the tree causing it not to produce fruit, but in further study I learned that the roots of a fig tree usually grow aerial, in the air, vertically downward from the branches. Once the roots are established they thicken which causes the tree to look as if it is supported by pillars. The roots are usually visible—spreading continuously, almost never ending.

In addition, the roots of a fig tree are so strong that if the seed of a fig tree starts to grow near another tree, the roots of the fig tree will grow around the other tree crushing the bark and killing the other tree.

This leads me to believe that the roots of the fig tree were visible to Jesus. Consequently, there would be no need to curse the roots of the tree if Jesus saw that they were already dead. Yet, the tree had a serious enough problem which caused it not to produce fruit warranting Jesus' curse (it possibly bore the very fruit that Adam and Eve ate).

We can only speculate as to why the fig tree did not bear any fruit. The scripture says it was not the season for figs, yet the tree was full of foliage which is an indication that fruit is present. Regardless of the reason, what we do know is Jesus dealt with the heart of the matter; He cursed the fig tree at the root, making sure that the tree would never bear fruit again.

We do not see Jesus cursing vegetation anywhere else in the Gospels. How many others had been on this same road, seeing this same tree full of foliage, like Jesus, only to find no fruit? How disappointing is that to a person who is seriously hungry after walking a long distance...to come upon a food source, and then find no food?

The tree was deceptive just as satan was deceptive in the Garden of Eden. Jesus was setting things in place for what was to come. He was letting satan know that the end was near for him. I believe Jesus was stripping satan of his power to deceive.

He was letting the enemy know a new heart was on the horizon for man, and that man was getting ready to be restored to his rightful place in God. Thus giving man the ability to make right choices out of an authentic heart; a God perfected heart.

Understand that we perceive everything through our hearts. This is how and where the issues in our lives are processed. Just like the fig tree whose roots grow strong and continuous, so do the emotional issues in our lives. If these issues are not properly processed, our hearts become burdened with unholy, deeply rooted emotions; and when others come to take of our fruit thinking it is good to eat, what they find is fruit that is bitter and full of anger and we are placed back in the Garden of Eden deceiving not just ourselves, but others as well.

The soul (mind, will, emotions), which is what impacts our hearts, must be transformed quickly to weed out offenses that try to set up root systems in our hearts. The time to weed is when we first recognize an offense has taken place; however, we are not always aware of the offense until someone or something triggers a negative response or emotion. Once that trigger clicks, we need to immediately begin asking the Holy Spirit to reveal the root cause of the offense. Upon knowing the root cause, we are able to take the Word of God and declare what the Word says—uprooting everything in us that is not like God.

Most offenses can be worked out by ourselves with the help of the Holy Spirit. However, there are some offenses that require us to approach those whom we believe we've offended or who have offended us. I have learned over the years that most offenses are a result of our own perceptions, and although our perceptions can be very real to us, it does not necessarily make them true.

Regardless if our perceptions are real or imagined, we must acknowledge those perceptions that cause us pain or negative thoughts. We should not let long periods of time go by, giving the issues time to fester in our hearts. The longer we go without confronting issues of the heart, the deeper the roots of the emotional pain; and the deeper the roots, the more time needed to uproot the negative emotions. Someone once told me that if it takes longer than three hours to resolve an issue in my heart, I should find someone to pray for me.

Fortunately, we can depend on the Holy Spirit to help us as we take steps to unmask these hidden areas. John 14:16-17 calls the Holy Spirit our helper who will show us the truth at the pace acceptable to our hearts. He, the Holy Spirit, will not overload us, or move us faster than we are ready. He will guide our hearts at a pace in which we can repent and forgive all those who have offended and caused us pain.

2

The Wounded Heart

In Luke 17:1 Jesus says, "It is impossible that no offenses should come." Here, Jesus is telling us we will have offenses; however, how we respond to these offenses is important in guarding our hearts from negative emotions. Some time ago, I burned myself while cooking, and the burn was right on the surface. There was no pain, and it was a very short healing process.

This is how we want to be when offenses come, and this can be done when we do not allow hurt feelings to inflame an offense. Offenses sometimes bring on hurt feelings, but those hurt feelings do not have to turn into feelings of anger and bitterness. At some time or another we all go through disappointments; however, when disappointments take us down to despair and defeat, we must stop and ask ourselves what the cause of our frustration and anger is. Years ago I was shopping, and upon opening the door to place packages in the car, the corner of the door hit my face right above my left eye causing it to bleed profusely. After controlling the bleeding, I looked in the mirror, and I could see that the cut was deep. I immediately realized that the wound needed to be closed so I headed to the closest hospital. There's still a small scar on my face from the incident.

We go through a similar process as we allow the Lord to go in and open up those areas of our wounded hearts that have been hidden for years. I remember while the wound was bleeding and unattended, it did not hurt. However, when I began to put pressure on it and attempted to control the bleeding, and when the doctors deadened the wound to prepare it to be stitched, the pain was great.

Like a physical wound, an emotional wound requires attention; and when left unattended, the emotional wound can build up layers of pain causing us to take on these negative emotions. Fortunately, we do have control over our emotions. We control whether or not we allow an offense to enter into our hearts from our soul-inciting wounds. We may experience some pain from the offense, but we decide whether or not that pain becomes imbedded, influencing our hearts negatively.

When we allow these emotional wounds to fester and set up roots inside our hearts, a root system is formed. This root system can bring bitterness, anger, resentment, hatred, mistrust, and other negative emotions that cause our flesh to rule over our spirits. This is why we need to forgive quickly. When we are not able to forgive, negative emotions begin to control us causing the heart to be hardened.

Forgiveness is not a choice for believers, it is a command. We are commanded to forgive even those who hurt and cause wounds in our emotions. I recognize that this may be hard to do, especially when you are presently experiencing pain. Consequently, we may even need to remove ourselves from an environment in order to start the healing process.

This is what I had to do. When the pain is a result of any type of abuse, healing can be short lived if the environment does not change. God never intended for us to live with abuse of any kind. In fact, Jesus took our abuse upon

> Abuse should be something that we never experience.

Himself on the Cross; therefore, it should be foreign to us. Abuse should be something that we never experience.

First Peter 4:14a tells us we will suffer for Christ's sake; "If you are reproached for the name of Christ, blessed are you, for the Spirit of glory and of God rests upon you." However, any other suffering is illegitimate to the believer.

We must allow the Holy Spirit to change us on the inside so that our emotions and behavior do not reflect what the person has done. This is not easy; yet, Jesus went to the cross and "was delivered up because of our offenses" (Romans 4:25). Christ took upon Himself all the sin of mankind, and when He arose, all mankind's sins were gone.

When we do not forgive, sin lingers, making it harder to forgive; and oftentimes this lingering sin requires the ministry of deliverance in order for us to be whole in our emotions again. It is a conscious decision to emotionally forgive, forget, and release a person who caused pain which brought about deep wounds. Prior to marrying Pastor Fred, Senior Pastor of the church we founded, I experienced a great deal of negative emotions in a relationship which led to depression.

The deliverance from God was instant because God is a right now God. However, the changing of the old mind set was a three-year process. I needed to totally remove myself from the negative environment, and let God unravel the layers of pain in every emotion that was not like Him, and renew my mind with His Word.

During this time period, the Lord showed me how angry and bitter I had become as a result of staying in this emotionally abusive relationship. I began to recognize how afraid I had become to face even the smallest decisions. As a result of hiding and not admitting the pain I was experiencing, these negative emotions literally took over my life.

It was not until I began to understand the power of forgiveness, what I now understand to be two-fold, that healing in my heart began to manifest. The first being His forgiveness of my sins, and the second being His grace (His ability) helping me to forgive all who offended and wounded me. What an amazing God we serve!

However, some years later, a friend explained that in forgiving, we also must release those who offended and wounded us. As she spoke, I sensed a witness in my spirit, and as soon as I was alone with God, I began to release people. How do you release someone who has wounded you?

If our forgiveness is a work of the flesh, which means we know it is the right thing to do, yet the heart is far from what is being done, this causes no change to take place and we are fooling ourselves. However, when we allow the Word of God to help us as it says in Hebrew 4:16, "Let us therefore come boldly to the throne of grace, that we may obtain mercy and find grace to help in time of need," the heart gravitates toward the Word, and begins to fill up with the Word of God until it is fully persuaded.

To assist the heart in becoming fully persuaded there are nine characteristics of God that give us a glimpse of His attributes that can help us release those that have wounded us. When we received Jesus Christ as our personal Savior and Lord, we received His love, and in His love rest all of His characteristics.

Consequently, we have what we need to combat the negative emotions, because we received God's character in the "new birth" experience. "As His divine power has given to us all things that pertain to life and godliness, through the knowledge of Him who called us by glory and virtue" (2Peter 1:3). God has given us the "fruit of the Spirit," positive emotions, to replace the negative emotions in our lives.

Prior to being born again, we had fruit, but it was negative fruit and was unpleasant to eat. We lived and responded with the fruit from the world.

> *Now the works of the flesh are evident, which are: adultery, fornication, uncleanness, lewdness, idolatry, sorcery, hatred, contentions, jealousies, outbursts of wrath, selfish ambitions, dissensions, heresies, envy, murders, drunkenness, revelries, and the like* (Galatians 5:19-21a).

When the heart is full of the Word of God, the circumstances that occur in life that filter through our souls (mind, will, emotions) will only find the "fruit of the Spirit" available.

But the fruit of the Spirit is love, joy, peace, longsuffering, kindness, goodness, faithfulness, gentleness, self-control, against such there is no law (Galatians 5:22-23).

Our understanding and willingness to allow God's character to operate in us helps us to forgive those who have hurt and wounded us in the past, and also helps us to forgive quicker when offenses come. We must let the "fruit of the Spirit" work in us showing us how to forgive.

Love

In John 3:16 we see God's love being demonstrated.

For God so loved the world that He gave His only begotten Son, that whosoever believes in Him should not perish but have everlasting life.

God's love deliberately sent His Son to die on the Cross to restore us back to Himself.

This kind of love is an act of giving that shows the true character of God Almighty. It is God's love in action, and He has given us His grace so we too can do what Philippians 2:3 tells us: "Esteem others better than ourselves" so when the offenses come, they will not set up negative fruit in our emotions.

Joy

"Rejoice in the Lord always and again I will say rejoice"
(Philippians 4:4).

We are to have gladness of heart always at all times. This word joy is the same word in James 1:2: "My brethren count it all joy when you fall into various trials."

We are to let joy lead and rule our hearts even during the most difficult times. The benefits of joy are for you personally. It is joy that will strengthen you from the inside out. Joy is pleasant, but not necessarily verbal. You can have quiet joy and contentment of heart or loud cheerful joy, but either way real joy comes from the Spirit of God. This kind of joy goes beyond the circumstances, and focuses on what God's Word says. It is a joy that is not always understood by those who may be aware of your circumstances, yet it is a joy that always brings peace.

Peace

And the peace of God, which surpasses all understanding,
will guard your hearts and minds through Christ Jesus
(Philippians 4:7).

Peace is rest with the absence of strife. When we have the peace of God we are not troubled or bothered in our emotions by the issues of life.

We recognize that the issues exist and we are not in denial, but the issues do not dominate our behavior. This does not mean negative thoughts will not try to come, but these thoughts are now combated with peace. There is tranquility and assurance that takes over in our emotions, and when this tranquility is present we are less likely to waver. We readily trust God, and we have a peaceful attitude to do what has been revealed to us by Him.

Longsuffering

"But in all things we commend ourselves as ministers of God: in much patience, in tribulations, in needs, in distresses" (2 Corinthians 6:4a).

We are to restrain ourselves in both body and mind. Although we may desire to avenge, God tells us to exercise patience.

Patience can go a long way to harness our emotions. It gives us strength to endure with a forgiving heart during difficult circumstances, for Ephesians 4:32 tells us, "And be kind to one another, tenderhearted, forgiving one another, even as God in Christ forgave you." Longsuffering moves you beyond tolerating a person. To tolerate someone means to put up with that person because it is politically correct or the right thing to do, yet the heart is not fully persuaded. I never want to feel as though someone is tolerating me. Longsuffering is an act of patiently waiting and extending the same mercy God extends. Doing so demonstrates the same compassion Jesus had for all mankind on the Cross. It is a patient waiting for the saved and the unsaved.

> Longsuffering moves you beyond tolerating a person.

Kindness

"That in the ages to come He might show the exceeding riches of His grace in His kindness toward us in Christ Jesus" (Ephesians 2:7).

This is the fruit of the Spirit that softens our character. It is seen in how we treat others. The best example I can give is God's kindness shown toward us through His grace.

Jesus' kindness, though we did not deserve it, gives us the results of God's grace—unmerited favor. It is shown towards us regardless of how we act. God does not take back His kindness because of our actions; we relinquish God's kindness because of our actions. His loving kindness draws us back to Him. "I will betroth you to Me forever. Yes, I will betroth you to Me in righteousness and justice, in loving kindness and mercy" (Hosea 2:19).

God is still kind toward us even during times of correction, and we need to practice this same virtue. Kindness can be shown in many ways including walking away from arguments which only lead to pain, and more importantly separate us from God. Jesus showed kindness in dying on the Cross, and we must do the same towards others.

We cannot duplicate what Christ did on the Cross, but we can die to self. We can decide not to be self-willed trying to control everything and everyone; and we too can let the love of God be seen in our kindness toward one another. This only requires a decision coupled with a committed heart.

Goodness

Then Jesus went into the temple of God and drove out all those who bought and sold in the temple, and overturned the tables of the money changers and the seats of those who sold doves. And He said to them, "It is written, 'My house shall be called a house of prayer,' but you have made it "a den of thieves' " (Matthew 21:12-13).

Here we see the goodness of Christ through His righteous indignation towards those selling in the temple. Where kindness shows our gentle nature, goodness shows our love while not sparing correction when necessary.

Within God's goodness is His righteousness, justice, kindness, grace, mercy, holiness, love, and His perfection; "Therefore you shall be perfect just as your Father in heaven is perfect" (Matthew 5:48). We do not have to strive to be perfect; we are declared perfect in Him. Nothing we can do will ever be good enough to make us righteous. We are declared righteous by a Holy God because of the finished work by Christ on the Cross. "By one Man's obedience many will be made righteous" (Romans 5:19b).

Faithfulness

"If we confess our sins, He is faithful and just to forgive us our sins and to cleanse us from all unrighteousness" (1 John 1:9).

Jesus is not only kind and good, He is faithful.

Often times this scripture is used to pray salvation; however, the Apostle John was speaking to the church when He wrote this scripture. Here, John is letting us know that God loves us so much even if we sin His forgiveness is always there.

I could tell numerous stories of the faithfulness of God in my life, but it would take the rest of the book and more. God is, and always will be faithful. "In hope of eternal life which God who cannot lie, promised before time began" (Titus 1:2). Unlike man He does not change for "with whom there is no variation or shadow of turning" (James 1:17b).

It is sad to say, but most of us tend to move in whatever direction the wind blows. The negative emotions out of which we function sometimes cause us to be "up" one day and "down" the next. "Beloved," this is not God's best. He wants us to trust Him, and use His Word to bring change in our emotions.

Renewing your mind will help you have trust in God. God cannot lie, and Isaiah 55:11 tells us, "So shall My Word be that goes forth from My mouth. It shall not return to Me void, but it shall accomplish what I please in the thing for which I sent it." The Word of God is "health (medicine) to all our flesh" (Proverbs 4:22b). Take the Word, saturate your heart with it (just as you would with medicine for your physical body), and watch the faithfulness of God's Word manifest in your life.

Trusting in the faithfulness of God's Word will illuminate the light of Christ in your heart. First John 1:5 says, "This is the message which we have heard from Him and declare to you, that God is light and in Him is no darkness at all." This light that is already in you does not go out; however, the light can become hidden when our hearts are full of negative characteristics because of wrong attitudes, motives and actions.

We do not lose what God has done in our hearts, but we can relinquish what was done in our hearts and make misguided decisions. If we do so, we're walking away from our trust and confidence in Him. During the times when our behavior or emotions are not like God's, this is the time we should draw close to Him, and trust in His faithfulness to see us through the circumstance.

Gentleness

And when they had come to him, he said to them: "You know, from the first day that I came to Asia, in what manner I always lived among you, serving the Lord with all humility, with many tears and trials which happened to me by the plotting of the Jews; how I kept back nothing that was helpful, but proclaimed it to you, and taught you publicly and from house to house" (Acts 20:18-20).

Here, we see the fruit of gentleness operating through the Apostle Paul who was encountering all types of trials, "who in labors more abundant, in stripes above measure, in prisons more frequently, in deaths often" (2 Corinthians 11:23b). Although Paul suffered greatly for the cause of Christ, he never seemed to forget the call on his life.

The Jews wanted to kill Paul after he preached in the synagogues in Damascus. His preaching caused amazement and horror to the Jews because earlier, Paul had been sent to

Damascus by the high priest to bind and bring all followers of Christ to Jerusalem (Acts 9:2). He suffered and was rejected when he tried to join the disciples in Jerusalem (Acts 9:26); he was beaten and put in prison in Philippi (Acts 16), and he was also severely beaten, put in prison, and made to stand before the Sadducees and Pharisees in Jerusalem (Acts 22-23).

I could go on and on, but you can find these and other accounts of Paul suffering for Christ, in the Book of Acts. Paul refused to allow the issues of life to cause him to lose focus of what God's plans were for his life. He moved forward even in the most difficult situations.

This did not mean that the Paul was timid; in fact, this fruit, when used, is quite the opposite of timidity. Self confidence is shown when we are in control of ourselves, as opposed to irrational outbursts that can lead to uncontrollable arguments which affect our emotions in a negative manner.

We must understand, when we allow the negative issues of life to dominate our emotions, we unknowingly lose focus on what God has for us to accomplish. An attitude of humility can make all the difference in the midst of a storm. This type of attitude can bring resolve and the favor of the Lord with your worst enemy. "A soft answer turns away wrath, but a harsh word stirs up anger" (Proverbs 15:1).

Self-Control

The last fruit of the Spirit is self-control which simply means you exhibit self-restraint in your conduct; you do not waver in your thoughts or your actions.

But also for this very reason, giving all diligence, add to your faith virtue, to virtue knowledge, to knowledge self-control, to self-control perseverance, to perseverance godliness, to godliness brotherly kindness, and to brotherly kindness love (2 Peter 1:5-7).

We are to be governed by God, not by self. We are able to control our emotions with God's grace which is His ability on the inside of us helping us to do what we are unable to do ourselves.

God's grace is His ability inside us.

This is a definition that I learned from one of the most profound books on God's grace I have ever read: *Grace The Power to Change*, by Dr. James Richards. It is a book I strongly recommend that you read regardless of how many years you have been saved.

We are nothing outside of Christ. All that we are and ever will be is because of His grace toward us and in us. I learned in reading this book that God's grace is not just unmerited favor. Unmerited favor is what we receive from God's grace. It is the by product. God's grace is His ability inside us. We no longer have to depend upon ourselves to make things happen or bring about change; we can believe in and trust in God's grace to bring the change.

We can continuously receive God's grace, His ability working in us, as long as we put our trust in Him and not in ourselves. I used to think this walk in Christ was impossible, and it is in "self," but it is not in Him. "For in Him we live and move and have our being" (Acts 17:28a).

Even during those times where self-restraint may be difficult, we can call upon God's grace.

> *For out of His fullness (abundance) we have all received [all had a share and we were all supplied with] one grace after another and spiritual blessing upon spiritual blessing and even favor upon favor and gift [heaped] upon gift"* (John 1:16 Amp.).

Again, the question is: How do we release those who have deliberately hurt and wounded us in our emotions? We release them through forgiveness, and by allowing the fruit of the Spirit to take over our emotions. Love, joy, peace, longsuffering, kindness, goodness, faithfulness, gentleness, self-control can supersede the negative emotions, and cause you to function in the manner God intended.

3

The Emotional Heart

In addition to the "fruit of the Spirit," Proverbs tells us "keep your heart with all diligence, for out of it spring the issues of life" (Proverbs 4:23). The heart is like a garden, and just like a garden the heart must be weeded if it is to function in the manner God designed. It must be maintained, inspected, kept, and watched. There are times when gardens even need to be protected from outside predators in order to protect the crop.

Since most gardens are open, they become prey to all types of things, some good and some bad. So it is with the heart; it filters everything that comes in through the soul. It is the path that leads us to fulfill our destiny in Christ, or the path that will lead us to destruction. You decide which road you will take.

Sometimes people try and dull the pain in the heart by filtering in drugs and alcohol through the pathway of the soul; however, once the stimuli wears off, the heart is right back where it started—in pain.

Emotional pain in the heart must be healed just as physical pain in the heart must be healed. We would never knowingly leave our physical heart, which is in pain, unattended. In fact, the sooner the damaged physical heart is medically attended, the greater the chance for a full recovery.

It is the same with our emotional hearts. The sooner we deal with the emotional issues that cause us pain, the faster healing will come. I neglected to deal with my issues at the appropriate time allowing a really destructive relationship to continue when I should have cut the relationship off. It was a wrong choice to remain in an emotionally abusive relationship. Unfortunately, some believers make these types of decisions in attempts to keep their families together.

> God never intended for us to endure any form of abuse in attempts to keep a family together.

"Beloved," God never intended for us to endure any form of abuse in attempts to keep a family together. All forms of abuse are from satan and should not be tolerated, whether male or female.

However, what God instructs us to do is live in peace. My environment at that time was far from peaceful, yet I continued in the environment. I want to emphasize that I continued in the environment. It was a choice I made although it was a bad choice. As a result of that choice, it took its toll on my emotions leaving me with a seriously wounded heart.

What is important to understand is when emotional pain is left to fester in the heart year after year, just like when a painful physical heart is left unattended; it can cause your life to spiral down, affecting you mentally and physically. This downward spiral, if not rescued with the Word of God, can lead to an emotional breakdown taking away your ability to function in your normal everyday life, affecting your every thought.

Regardless if we are awake or asleep, our minds are going to think on something; therefore, we should train our minds to think on the Word of God. No longer should we allow anything outside of God's Word to have place in our hearts or our thoughts, because the only thing that is true in this world is the Word of God. When we allow the Holy Spirit to fill our hearts with the Word, there will be no more room for any negative emotions. The heart will be full of God's emotions—His character.

With the Word of God, we can make decisions without trying to control the circumstances. Our emotions will no longer dictate; but instead, will come in line with what our spirit dictates. Our judgments in making decisions will no longer depend on our emotional opinions, but will pull from the wisdom of God according to James 1:5, "If any of you lacks wisdom, let him ask of God, who gives to all liberally and without reproach, and it will be given to him." You will ask God for His wisdom with full expectation that He will give you exactly what you requested of Him.

When we meditate on the Word on a daily basis, and offenses come, these offenses will not be able to stay. I cannot stress enough the importance of combating these negative emotions with the Word of God. The Amplified Bible tells us, "For the Word that God speaks is alive and full of power making it active, operative, energizing and effective; it is sharper than any two edged sword, penetrating to the dividing line of the breath of life (soul) and the immortal spirit, and of joints and marrow of the deepest parts of our nature, exposing and sifting and analyzing and judging the very thoughts and purposes of the heart" (Hebrew 4:12).

This tells us there is nothing that we will ever experience that the Word of God cannot fix if we renew our minds, removing all negative thoughts with the power of God's Word. Again, it bears repeating: Christianity is what we allow God to do in us on the inside, in our hearts, continuously changing us from glory to glory.

Another area that brings about emotional hiding is what Pastor Fred calls "the blame game." Intentionally or unintentionally, many times we tend to blame others for our negative emotions disguised as problems, when in reality our behavior is the culprit. Accepting responsibility for our own choices, even the bad choices, removes us from the blame game. It brings us to a place where we can finally move forward.

Once we accept responsibility, we need to forgive ourselves for making the decision the world's way instead of God's way. It is wrong to hold ourselves hostage to bad decisions even when we think we do not deserve God's forgiveness. Know that it is satan trying to convince your heart that you are not worthy to be forgiven, and the Word instructs us that satan is defeated and under our feet.

Yes, there are consequences to bad decisions, but even God forgives and forgets. We cannot allow pride to hinder even forgiving ourselves; therefore, we must forgive ourselves, and then make a decision not to repeat the behavior.

Another way we bring pain upon ourselves is when we have expectations of others, and those expectations do not measure up to our beliefs. Do not let your expectations of others become a stumbling block, discarding people when they do not meet your approval. It is not wrong to want people to excel, but there is a balance between healthy expectations and codependent expectations.

Codependent behavior is our emotional expectations towards others. It is an emotional behavioral pattern that chronically attempts to please, manipulate or control others. The codependent person does not ask for their needs to be met directly, but they choose to go along with the inappropriate behavior in an effort to meet their emotional needs.

> Codependent behavior is our emotional expectations towards others.

The term was originally used to describe wrong behavior in alcoholic, drug, and chemical dependent relationships; however, the term is presently used to describe any relationship where emotional pain and shame is ignored or denied.

Signs of codependent behavior include, but are not limited to: low self-esteem, looking for something or someone to make us feel good about ourselves and finding it hard to be who God created us to be. Often, codependent behavior may cause compulsive behavior such as constantly trying to change someone or something, gambling, over working or always trying to save or take care of others experiencing difficulty in our efforts. Most of these tendencies are hidden in the honorable guises of "trying to help or doing what we believe to be right," in truth, they become obsessive and usually self-defeating.

When we operate out of codependent behavior, and try to

manipulate and control others, our hearts become so covered that no one truly gets to know us, the real us. We put on false appearances trying to convince others that our lives are perfect, when deep inside our hearts we are miserable. We also try to change others instead of allowing the Word of God to change our lives so others can see Christ in us through our behavior.

Have you ever been around someone who seemed very distant and guarded in their mannerisms? You really would enjoy a closer relationship with the person, but they do not allow you to get emotionally close. This type of behavior usually reflects where the person is in their heart.

I have found that people often act in this manner out of fear of being rejected concerning themselves with what others think about them. You might be surprised to know that most people have their own problems, and they really do not spend a lot of time thinking about the problems of others. Most people will willingly admit that their lives require more attention than they can handle.

Sure, letting our guard down and revealing more of our true self means taking a risk and becoming vulnerable; but it also means we are more likely to be real with God, thus putting a stop to the hiding of our emotions (unlike Adam, and Eve). "And they heard the sound of the Lord God walking in the garden in the cool of the day, and Adam and his wife hid themselves from the presence of the Lord God among the trees of the garden" (Genesis 3:8).

Note that when Adam and Eve hid themselves, in their minds it was an attempt to hide their physical bodies; instead, they ended up hiding from the presence of the Lord. They now had knowledge of both good and evil. Prior to their disobedience they only knew "good."

They experience shame and separation from God for the first time thus sensing that something was different. In the beginning they were clothed in God's Glory, so no physical clothing was needed, but once the glory lifted they knew they were naked. So it is with us when we hide, the condition in our heart controls how God's grace operates in our lives – in that we also feel naked.

Yes, we think we are hiding from others, but in reality we have hidden, like Adam and Eve, from the presence of God. We are responding in the same manner as Adam and Eve. Job 32:33 tells us, "If I have covered my transgressions as Adam, by hiding my iniquity in my bosom." The word bosom here means to cherish.

I remember when I was a child, my mother would hide her money in a handkerchief and pin it inside her bra. Because she cherished what was in the handkerchief she would hide it in her bosom to keep from losing it. Similarly, we do the same thing when our hearts are hidden. We unknowingly cherish the negative emotions, and we hold on to them when we should be releasing and letting them go.

Adam and Eve were attempting to cover the willful disobedience of what God had instructed. The choice they made to eat the forbidden fruit bought wickedness and rebellion into the whole world. Their disobedience gave satan the legal right to try and destroy the man God had created.

Adam and Eve experienced immediate fear after their disobedience. "So he said, I heard Your voice in the garden, and I was afraid because I was naked; and I hid myself" (Genesis 3:10).

They were paralyzed and not knowing what to do, they hid. Can you see Adam and Eve crouched down on their knees trying to hide from God? And, sadly, they did not even realize how satan had deceived them and caused their hearts to no longer experience the presence of the Lord.

Fortunately for us, there is good news! The blood of Jesus has removed all of the deception giving us authority over the enemy and bringing us into the Kingdom of God. "Beloved," kingdom living is not for when we get to Heaven. We won't need it in Heaven for everything in Heaven is perfect; it is for the here and now that we need kingdom living because the Kingdom of God is within you right now. Romans 14:17 tells us: "For the kingdom of God is not eating and drinking, but righteousness and peace and joy in the Holy Spirit."

This kingdom living is righteousness which means you are totally accepted by God now and forever more. This righteousness has nothing to do with our past or our future. We are declared righteous in Him (Christ), and it is settled in Heaven and on Earth.

This kingdom living is "peace" in knowing that "it is finished" (John 19:30). Everything is done; Jesus did it all. We cannot add anything to, nor can we take away from, the finished work of Christ.

This kingdom living is "joy" in knowing our Redeemer lives, and He "Jesus Christ is the same yesterday, today and forever" (Hebrew 13:8). He can never be taken away, and He will never leave us. We must understand this for righteousness is the foundation of all that we believe.

When our hearts are covered with life's issues, hiding us from

God's presence, we are hidden from all that He is in our lives; all of His attributes. Some of God's attributes are: Creator of all things (Nehemiah 9:6); His works unsearchable (Ecclesiastes 8:17); Wisdom (Romans 16:27); To be loved (Matthew 22:37); His presence (Ezekiel 43:1); His goodness (Psalms 86:5); His holiness (Isaiah 6:3); His majesty (Habakkuk 3:3); None beside Him (Deuteronomy 4:35); His love to Christians (1 John 3:1); The One who heals (Exodus 15:26); To be imitated (Ephesians 5:1); True God (Jeremiah 10:10); His immortality (Deuteronomy 33:27). We should want to see God's attributes operate in our lives.

When our heart is covered, we cannot receive from God's attributes nor do circumstances work out to our benefit. This is because the truth is being hidden. How can the truth spring forth in a hidden heart? Yes, God will come to our aid, but the hidden heart will only receive in part. We need to be

> How can the truth spring forth in a hidden heart?

open in our hearts if we want all that God has to offer.

Imagine. Here is Adam in the garden hiding from his Creator who he was used to talking with on a regular basis. It was as though Adam physically died. He could no longer fellowship with God as he was accustomed. He could no longer walk in the garden with God, nor could he talk with God about His next plan for man. Adam was no longer privileged to receive information I believe the Spirit of God revealed to him on a regular basis, keeping him informed of God's next move for him and his family.

All of that was gone, and he would never be able to get back what he lost; how sad. He moved from hanging out with his

Creator to hiding from his Creator. Adam knew that something was now different; he was no longer like his Father because his body immediately became imperfect and corruptible. He felt shame and physical pain for the first time.

This is why God had to come to Earth as a man. Jesus had to redeem mankind and bring man back to God's original plan, and although man failed, God's love for man did not change, nor did God's plan for man change. Thank God, Jesus willingly and obediently finished His assignment given to Him by the Father. Jesus experienced the pain and the shame of the Cross for us. Where we probably would have given up, He refused to give up. He accomplished all that was expected of Him.

Now, here we are. Jesus does a complete work in our hearts only for us to allow the issues of life to bring such profound negative emotions causing us to function as though we were never saved. "Beloved," Christ has done all that He is going to do. Now we must do something about these negative emotions that have taken control of our hearts. We must use the Word of God to renew our minds.

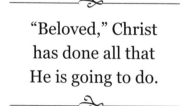

"Beloved," Christ has done all that He is going to do.

The Word of God has been given to the believer to live by. However, what the Church has done is lived out of the "gifts of the spirit" with no character change in the soul. Let me explain. Christianity is supposed to produce change in our character and cause our souls to come in line with our spirits. It is more important to see the character of Christ in us through the fruit of the Spirit than it is for us to move and flow in the "gifts of the

Spirit with no fruit." We move and flow in the gifts out of the anointing of the Holy Spirit; however, when the anointing lifts, it is our character that is left, and our character is a product of what is in our hearts.

This is why Jesus was sent. Man's character was no longer like God. It is unacceptable for us to make excuses for bad dispositions and behavior blaming it on our personalities or using the excuse, "This is how I am; I have always been this way."

We must now deprogram all of the negative thoughts in our minds that are holding us back. Our minds are similar to an old fashioned record that was used to play music on a phonograph. The record was designed with grooves going in one direction so you had to put the record on the phonograph correctly for it to play. So it is with our minds. It has been programmed to go in one direction, but we can renew our minds with the Word of God and reverse the old mindset. When we renew our minds, all of the negative emotions will be deleted making new grooves and, literally changing how we think.

Renewing the mind is fundamental for all believers if we want to live the abundant life that Jesus speaks about. We must function out of the right heart, and only God's Word can bring consistent change to our hearts. Jesus was not just concerned with the truth; He was concerned about the motivation behind the truth. He came to bring lasting change in our hearts; a change that the world needed to see.

4

Five Reasons Why We do not
Relinquish Wounds of the Heart

Let us look at five areas: fear, denial, confusion in the mind, forgiveness, and past emotional pain that cause us not to relinquish wounds of the heart. Although we may be aware of something not being quite right in our hearts, we are not always aware that we are hiding, leaving us feeling helpless and unable to explain why we feel as we do. For example: I remember feeling hurt and alone, but I do not remember thinking the root of my problem was a result of my own emotional issues. However, once I understood where the pain was coming from, I knew I had to make changes in my life if I wanted to be free.

Fear

The first emotion that we need to look at is fear, "For God has not given us a spirit of fear, but power and of love and of a sound mind" (2 Timothy 1:7).

This scripture clearly lets us know that we are dealing with a spirit. When and where did this spirit first begin to operate through man? Genesis 3:10 gives us our answer. "Adam said to God, I heard your voice in the garden, and I was afraid because I was naked, and I hid myself." It was in the garden. This was Adam's emotions responding to what his heart was now saying. His emotions now had control over his spirit for the first time, and he perceived harm which was something his heart had never experienced. His perceptions became his reality.

Fear brings us into a condition or behavior pattern of helplessness or inactivity. It can also bring us into a place of self-hatred. It causes us to feel paralyzed and powerless as though we are no longer in control of our fate; fear is now in control, causing us to hide because we do not want our true self to be revealed to others.

Picture this. Up until this time, Adam had it made. He was created to be just like God, and he communicated with his God, and God shared His plan for man with him. There was nothing God kept from Adam. Adam was "the man," and God blessed them in the Garden of Eden and told them to be fruitful and multiply (Genesis 128a). God was pleased with His creation.

Now here is Adam, the one God created to be just like Himself, taking matters into his own hands, bringing fear into the earth. Adam's eyes were now opened to both good and evil, and this new knowledge gripped his heart and caused him to hide from the presence of God.

I believe Adam knew instantly the relationship which he had enjoyed with his God was now over, changed, with the change being so profound, he covered himself with fig leaves not even realizing that his physical body was not the problem; it was his heart that was the problem. His relationship with God would never be the same.

Unfortunately, we still today go about making our own decisions without asking God about His plans for us. How many times have we made a decision, and then asked God for His blessing after the fact? This is what Adam and Eve did. What a horrible place to be in for Adam and Eve; a place where one can never be restored. Thank God for Jesus, "in that while we were still sinners, Christ died for us" (Romans 5:8b).

Fear is uneasiness and anxiousness, which occupies our thoughts, but before fear presents itself, doubt and unbelief always arrive on the scene first. We begin to doubt what God's Word says, and we begin functioning from the old heart instead of the new heart given to us in our new birth experience.

When fear is left to fester in our hearts, our behavior will send out red flags that we are experiencing inward challenges even if we are not aware that it is happening. The fear will wreak havoc in our emotions and our thoughts. Every decision we make will be made out of fear. Again, unless there is some type of medical problem, we are going to think on something. When fear is present, these thoughts are usually not godly. The thoughts tend to be focused on defeat instead of victory.

We must not let fear operate in our emotions. The spirit of fear is a trespasser that has no rights or authority; however, we choose whether or not we allow fear to operate and dominate our lives. If we do not fight against fear, the negative emotion will take control of our every thought.

"Finally my brethren, be strong in the Lord and in the power of His might. Put on the whole armor of God that you may be able to stand against the wiles of the devil. For we do not wrestle against flesh and blood, but against principalities, against powers, against the rulers of the darkness of this age, against spiritual host of wickedness in the heavenly places" (Ephesians 6:10-12).

The Word of God is the weapon to use to battle any demonic force. When we look at the life of Christ as satan tried to temp Him, Jesus responded with "It is written" (Matthew 4:4). We have been given that same authority to use the Word of God to shut the enemy down in our lives, and in our families' lives.

"Beloved," do not take this lightly. Read Genesis chapter one and two, "God spoke and it was." God was not just putting things into place in the heavens; He was showing us a principal of how things would work here on earth. He was showing us that even He was bound by His Word, and so is His Son. "In hope of eternal life which God, who cannot lie" (Titus 1:2a). He did exactly what He spoke. Learn to speak the Word of God continuously and watch fear leave your life as you stand on the Word of God.

Denial

The act of denial means to contradict or disown the truth causing us to become prideful. We refuse to accept that we have problems in our emotions, and we deny the pain because we do not want to appear weak, and we either do not know how, or choose not to forgive and release others because of pride. Proverbs 16:18 tells us "Pride goes before destruction and a haughty spirit before a fall."

Pride is not a personality issue, it is a character issue. When we are prideful, disowning the truth about ourselves, we often go through life with the mindset "life is good" and "everything is okay." When we are prideful, our character is saying we choose not to forgive and release those who have wounded us, and when

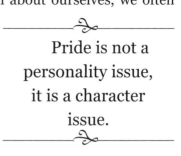

Pride is not a personality issue, it is a character issue.

our emotions try and tell us something different, we reject the appropriate thoughts and continue with what satisfies us in our emotions at that time.

I am reminded of Ananias and Sapphira in Acts 5:1-10. Here was a husband and wife who obviously were not poor, yet they denied the truth when asked about the sale of their property. What we need to look at is verse four; "While it remained, was it not your own? And after it was sold, was it not in your own control? Why have you conceived this thing in your heart? You have not lied to men but to God."

Notice where the problem was with Ananias; it was in his heart, and although Ananias was going about his day doing what he normally would do, he neglected one thing—to check the condition of his heart in giving to the work of God.

Read further verses 32-35 of Acts chapter five. "Now the multitude of those who believed was of one heart and one soul; neither did anyone say that any of the things he possessed was his own, but they had all things in common. Nor was there anyone among them who lacked; for all who were possessors of lands or houses sold them, and brought the proceeds of the things that were sold, and laid them at the apostles' feet; and they distributed to each as anyone had need."

Maybe Ananias was not present on the day the church agreed to make all things common, and he did not have knowledge of what was in verse thirty-two. I don't think that was the case. Ananias gave with the wrong heart and then denied the truth to try and justify his actions. What did it cost Ananias? It cost him his life along with the life of his wife.

You cannot afford to let denial rule your heart. It can cost you your spiritual life and maybe your physical life. If you know you are in denial about where you are in your heart, stop right now and repent, and trust God's grace to help you turn your heart back towards God. You will find Jesus with healing and deliverance waiting to embrace you.

Confusion in the Mind

The word confusion simply means disorder. Confusion means the mind is perplexed or our ideas and thoughts become mixed up. Recently I was talking with someone when I noticed, during the conversation, that the person seemed to be somewhat scattered in presenting her point of view. She never seemed to be able to complete a thought, and she would move from one topic to the next without ending the previous topic.

I was having a conversation, yet at the end of the conversation I had no idea what had been said. I tried to listen even more closely after detecting a problem, so I could respond appropriately. I found myself needing God's grace just to listen to her. I believe she was sincere, but the words from her thoughts just were not clear.

When the mind is confused, the conversation can be so

scattered you can find yourself asking what was the point that was being made. You just did not get it. Also, when a person talks all the time, that person's listening skills are usually poor. The person is talking and responding in their mind all at the same time. Instead of appropriately listening and then responding.

Also, when we are confused, we tend to question everything making the truth hard to see because we do not trust or have confidence in others. It is normal for us to question and we should, but everything? What we are truly saying knowingly or unknowingly is that we do not trust what God's Word says about us. We make excuses for our lack of trust, and we blame others for their short comings while we never look at our own short comings.

Another definition for confusion is: throwing thoughts together indiscriminately to where our thoughts are so jumbled it is hard for anyone to understand what we are saying. This can easily happen when we are anxious.

When we are anxious, our thoughts are focused on things that add no value to our lives. For example, we have a bill that is due, but we have no money to pay the bill. Does anything of value get added to our life because we have chosen to worry or be anxious as to how the bill will be paid? Of course the answer to this question is no. So, what we should do is speak what the Word says about the situation thus releasing our anxiousness.

What we think on is extremely important because what we think on affects our emotional behavior. Philippians 4:8 tells us, "whatever things are true, whatever things are noble, whatever things are just, whatever things, are pure, whatever things are lovely, whatever things are of a good report, if there is any virtue and if there is anything praise worthy, meditate on these things."

I have read this scripture many times over the years thinking I understood what it meant. I would always make sure that I was thinking on positive things, and not negative things. However, this is not what this scripture is saying. It was not until I heard a friend teach on this scripture that God began to show me more revelation.

There is only one thing that meets all of the criteria in Philippians 4:8 and that is the Word of God. So, no matter how positive our thinking is, only the Word of God is able to bring about change in our lives that will last.

Positive thinking without the Word can only bring limited success. It cannot bring heart-changing success, and it will not transform your heart. It can change your emotions, and even that change can be short lived especially if the positive thinking stops.

Therefore, this is saying:

- Whatever things are true— is the Word of God not true?

- Whatever things are noble— can you think of anything nobler than the Word of God, the noblest person you know does not compare in their ability to bring deliverance as the Word of God?

- Whatever things are just— the Word is just, notice it did not say fair (God is a just God, everything in life is not always fair, yet God is always just)

- Whatever things are pure— there are no preservatives in His Word (God's Word is pure)

- Whatever things are lovely—is not His Word acceptable and friendly toward us?

- Whatever things are of a good report— whose report should we believe? (we shall believe the report of the Lord for the Word of God is the report of the Lord)

- If there is any virtue—yes, His Word is excellent

- And if there is anything praiseworthy—yes, His Word is always commendable—meditate on these things.

Understand that confusion in the mind is strongly influenced by wrong thinking, and although satan may have a part in the confusion, most of the time, it is our own issues that bring the confusion. This is why we must meditate on the Word of God until change comes in the heart bringing wholeness to our souls.

Past Painful Emotions

It is painful to work through issues that deal with our emotions. No one enjoys going through any form of pain; however, again pain usually reveals that there is a problem. In addition, unresolved pain can bring about depression that presses down on the mind causing our heart to be covered.

Sometimes feelings of inadequacy arise out of depression. These inadequate feelings rest in our hearts. They cause us to feel as though we are not adequate or capable of making changes in our life. This is not someone who just had a bad day; this is someone whose thoughts are telling them they have no ability, no strength, no power, and no resources.

As I began to look at this closer, the only ability we truly have is what God has given us by His grace. His ability in us helps us to do what we are not able to do ourselves, "working in you what is well pleasing in His sight, through Christ Jesus" (Hebrews 13:21).

It is God's strength working in our hearts giving us the courage to continue. It is God's power through His Holy Spirit enabling us to boldly declare the Word of God over the circumstances, and it is the written Word of God that is our resource.

The written Word is our resource for every issue in our lives. Even when the resource, the Word of God, does not say what we want to hear; it is still true and it will still bring victory when we do what the Word tells us to do.

God gave us His Word to live by regardless of our circumstances. Therefore, we must use His resource for every area of our lives. We must study and meditate on the Word of God consistently because it is the only thing that will bring lasting change to our heart. The Word truly hidden in our hearts is our weapon to defeat the issues of life that come to steal our peace and our joy. It is what God gave us to bring change in our souls so that our souls look more and more like our spirits. Nothing else can do this. "Your word is a lamp to my feet and a light to my path" (Psalms 119:105).

Also, we must apply the Word in our daily walk, for to truly know a thing is to do it. You see, satan quoted the Word, but he could not apply what was not in his heart; he could not make it manifest. We can no longer live full of the Word in our conscious memory with no application of that same Word in our lives. Romans 12:2 tells us, "And do not be conformed to this world, but be transformed by the renewing of your mind, that you may prove what is the good, acceptable and perfect will of God."

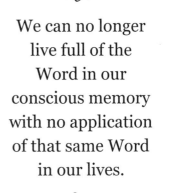

We can no longer live full of the Word in our conscious memory with no application of that same Word in our lives.

Pastor Fred talks about parrots that are excellent at mimicking what is said to them. They are diligent in their pursuit accomplishing, with great perseverance, the art of speaking what they hear. However, regardless of how well the parrot speaks, the parrot will never understand with any real significance what is being repeated. The parrot merely repeats what he hears.

This is the believer who sits in church for years and who is busy teaching, serving, and possibly preaching, yet never seems to enter into the depth of God's Word for themselves and in their own heart. They are just like the parrot. They can repeat the word with diligence, but have no application of the Word because they have not allowed the Word to produce change in their heart. It is only transformation in our heart that will cause us to live the abundant life God intends.

Forgiveness

Matthew 6:14-15 in the Amplified Bible gives us the strongest and clearest reason that we are to forgive even our enemies. "For if you forgive people their trespasses [their reckless and willful sins, leaving them, letting them go, and giving up resentment], your heavenly Father will also forgive you, but if you do not forgive others their trespasses [their reckless and willful sins, leaving them, letting them go, and giving up resentment], neither will your Father forgive you your trespasses."

This tells us even those things that are willfully done to us, we are to forgive, and show no resentment toward the guilty person. A good way to understand forgiveness is to truly understand God's grace toward us. When we confess Christ as our personal Savior, God no longer sees any of our wrong. He sees us redeemed, complete, whole and righteous. Looking at us is like looking at His Son. How awesome is that? We did nothing to deserve what He sees; it's just the way it is!

Therefore, if God no longer sees our sins or our past, what right do we have to not forgive those who have wounded us? "For sin shall not have dominion over you, for you are not under law but under grace" (Romans 6:14).

When we forgive, there is a peace that comes, and the peace causes us to see the person who wounded us differently. Although we do not have the power or the authority to forgive a person of sin, that power belongs to God alone, we do have the power to forgive the person of the wrong done to us.

The forgiving of those hurts done to us in the past is a choice we make. We can walk in a place of such forgiveness of past hurts to where there is no sting from the pain that was in the heart. The pain is no longer a part of our lives, and even our memory rejects the thought of any residue from the past.

Walking in this type of forgiveness must be done on a continuous basis. We must understand that it is not a one-time process if we want to be free from all contamination in our hearts. God can only bring about this type of healing as we surrender our hearts to Him daily. A heart surrendered to God is a choice we must make when we want to be free.

Letting the past go and not allowing it to rule or control our future or dominate what we do in the present is very important. "How do we get to this place?" is the question. When we are stuck in the past, we usually have not forgiven those who have wronged us. What is important to understand is that not forgiving those who have wronged us will cause the past to control the present and the future. This means our destiny is being controlled by something other than ourselves.

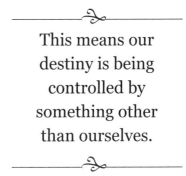

This means our destiny is being controlled by something other than ourselves.

Do we really want to give something or someone, other than God, control over our lives? Our answer should be no.

It is your choice whether or not to forgive someone who caused you pain. When you choose to forgive, the Holy Spirit will show you every negative emotion that has settled and rested in your heart if you truly desire to know. Then you can begin to understand why you respond in the manner that you do in certain situations.

The Holy Spirit will take you through healing and deliverance in your emotions revealing people from your past you need to forgive, and as you continue to let God work in your heart, you will begin to forgive quicker letting nothing ungodly fester in your heart.

Nonetheless, the Holy Spirit and the Word of God are here to help us combat these negative emotions if we surrender to Him. "And I will pray the Father and He will give you another Helper, that He may abide with you forever" (John 14:16); "However, when He the Spirit of truth has come, He will guide you into all truth; for He will not speak on His own authority, but whatever He hears He will speak; and He will tell you things to come" (John 16:13).

You must trust and depend on the Holy Spirit to show you those emotions in your heart that are not like God. He will show you revelation in the Word to help you bring closure to those issues that have invaded your heart. He knows what is in your heart at every second. In fact, the Holy Spirit knows what is in our hearts before it arrives in our heart. He has been given to us by Christ to live with us forever.

It is important to understand that you can only change yourself. Changes in others must come from their own decisions. Every day we make choices, and choosing not to change is a choice. You also need to know, it is okay to move forward even when others choose not to. Also, if you choose not to relinquish the past, most of the decisions you make knowingly or unknowingly will be made

> A wise decision in the now can save you time and pain in the latter.

from a hidden heart. Do not wait until the enemy attacks you with depression, physical sickness, or some other crisis before you decide to change. A wise decision in the now can save you time and pain in the latter.

The Word of the Lord is found in the Song of Solomon. "For lo, the winter is past, the rain is over and gone" (Song of Solomon 2:11). The word winter here means a dark hidden place, and rain here means to shower violently. What the Lord is saying to you today is those issues that were dark and violent in your past are over and gone.

The violent rain has passed; with God's grace (His ability in you) you can stop the negative emotions from controlling your decisions. Your life can be different to the point of not even having conversation about past issues. This may be hard for you to believe, but I do not have negative conversation about those that I have forgiven from my past. When I do speak about a person, it is usually a part of my testimony of how God has healed and delivered me from emotional pain from that relationship.

We must be honest with ourselves if we are not going to allow the past to control our future. I continue to learn how merciful God is and how His grace keeps me, and He still does not remind me of my past mistakes. Yet, we sometimes continue to remind ourselves of our past through our actions.

Let me explain what I mean. We cannot go to God and ask Him about something that we have already repented. God forgives us and He does not remember those things, "I will forgive their iniquity, and their sin I will remember no more" (Jeremiah 31:34).

So would you agree that we do not have the right to hold on to past hurts? This is not just those hurts from years ago, but those hurts or offenses from yesterday. The offenses that come on a daily basis are to be forgiven quickly. The same choice applies whether it was twenty years ago or today.

There is no difference between today and twenty years ago because today's hurts in our emotions are tomorrow's seeds of pain for the next twenty years. Therefore, it is a daily allowing of the Holy Spirit to search our heart for unresolved negative emotions.

Ask the Holy Spirit to search your heart everyday, and show you how and if you were offended in any manner. Many times we do not know that an offense has occurred until down the road something else that happens triggers an emotion about a particular incident. At that time, it is important to quickly repent and forgive that person and move on.

There is an amazing difference in our attitudes when we immediately forgive someone as opposed to harboring resentment for months. The difference being there is no lingering residue, and we do not allow negative roots to be set up in our emotions.

How important is it to forgive and move forward? Had I still been in that negative place in my emotions, I would not have been ready to receive the man I believe God always had for me. There would have been too much anger and bitterness that the man of God would have to wade through to get to the real me. Thank God I made a choice to let God heal my hidden heart. Let me add that I was not looking for a mate when God sent my husband, but I was ready to receive him in my emotions. Many times we are praying for a mate when we are not ready to receive.

Let us look at Philippians 3:12-14 where Paul is talking about pressing toward the goal. "Not that I have already attained, or am already perfected; but I press on, that I may lay hold of that for which Christ Jesus has also laid hold of me. Brethren, I do not count myself to have apprehended; but one thing I do, forgetting those things which are behind and reaching forward to those things which are ahead. I press toward the goal for the prize of the upward call of God in Christ Jesus."

Paul is telling the Philippians that he may not have it all together, but the one thing he knows he's on the ball about, is how he doesn't look back to the issues or events of the past to propel him forward. He goes so far as to say he forgets those things which I believe where things he did prior to his born again experience and things after his conversion. Regardless of your school of thought as to what Paul meant, he chose not to let the things in the past stop him from moving forward.

Just because we have made a mistake does not mean that God has changed His mind about the plans He has for us. His love toward us "is the same, yesterday, today, and forever" (Hebrews 13:8). We should expect to receive the very best from God all the time.

Yes, there are consequences to our actions, but the Word of the Lord for you today is "I have been young, and now am old; yet I have not seen the righteous forsaken, nor his descendants begging bread" (Psalms 37:25).

What God desires is for us not to continue in sin, and His grace gives us His ability to live a life without sin, repeating the same mistake over and over pulling us deeper into hiding. Do not think because you missed it in the past that your destiny will not come to pass!

God has already predestined your life, "In Him also we have obtained an inheritance, being predestined according to the purpose of Him who works all things according to the counsel of His will" (Ephesians 1:11).

Your future was laid out before the foundation of the world. Satan tries, however, to get you in a defeated state of mind of not trusting God. The enemy of your soul (satan) uses lies to try and convince you that your future is over. God says to you today, "Not so." He will never stop loving you, and it is God's desire to see you complete the work He has predestined.

There are also good things in our past that we should remember and hold on to. In fact, many of us have a heritage passed to us from our loved ones who were dedicated and served God whole heartedly. Paul talks about this heritage with Timothy. "I thank God, whom I serve with a pure conscience, as my forefathers did, as without ceasing I remember you in my prayers night and day, greatly desiring to see you, being mindful of your tears, that I may be filled with joy, when I call to remembrance the genuine faith that is in you, which dwelt first in your grandmother Lois and your mother Eunice, and I am persuaded is in you also" (1 Timothy 1:3-5).

Here, Paul is reminding Timothy of his heritage in Christ. Paul knew the issues that Timothy would face as a young pastor, so he was encouraging him not to be fearful, and to reach back and pull on the gifts that were already in him.

Paul also knew that reminding Timothy of his heritage would give him strength for the task ahead. The positive things from the past can be used to strengthen us while the negative things are used as preventive medicine. We should look back to thank

God for how far He has bought us allowing those things to be our testimony.

We should tell others of the goodness of God, and testify that this same God can and will do the same for them. "I will remember the work of the Lord" (Psalms 77:11). Go ahead and reflect, recollect, declare and proclaim those things from which God has delivered you, and

> Just understand that the past is a testimony, and not a memorial.

"Remember the days of old" (Psalms 143:5). Just understand that the past is a testimony, and not a memorial.

5

The Healed Heart

Let me begin by saying, forgiveness rules the healed heart. It is the foundation of what Christ did for us on the Cross. Had Christ not gone to the Cross and died for our past, present and future sins, our lives would be a continuous wandering in the wilderness just like the Israelites. Ephesians 4:32 tells us, "be kind to one another, tenderhearted, forgiving one another, even as God in Christ forgave you." The healed heart understands the mercy that was shown to man on the Cross, and willingly extends that same mercy.

Only trust in God can cause us to love just as Christ did all the way to the Cross of obedience. David tells us in Psalms 27:14, "Wait on the Lord; be of good courage, and He will strengthen your heart; wait I say, on the Lord." The healed heart will always follow after God because it trusts unconditionally in what the Word of the Lord says.

The waiting that David is speaking of is a trusting in the Lord;

faithfully trusting every Word God has spoken. This trusting brings a feeling of completeness in Christ to the heart because it is only moved by the Word, and does not surrender to fleshly emotions.

Trust is vital when developing godly relationships, and while we all have encountered trust issues with others, we still need to have a heart that is not hidden. Unfortunately, wounds from our past many times set up pain in our hearts to where we are not willing to trust. We end up living a life depending only on self.

Trust in self alone is ungodly behavior. God created man for relationship. Genesis 1:26a tells us, "Let Us make man in Our image, according to Our likeness." Genesis 2:7 goes on to say, "and the Lord God formed man out of the dust of the ground, and breathed into his nostrils the breath of life; and man became a living being."

God created both man and angels, but He only breathed life into man. The very essence of God was put into man. Now God had a being just like Himself with whom He could fellowship. God is so serious about relationships that He said, "It is not good that man should be alone" (Genesis 2:18). Then what would lead us to believe that we do not need one another when it was God who formed man, and then created the woman so that man would have someone like himself with whom to communicate?

Godly relationships are important because they can give us a place to go when we need sound counsel. It helps our minds be at ease to know there are people praying, and encouraging us in the things of God, helping to bring our hearts to maturity. It was not God's desire for man to be alone nor should it be ours, even if building relationships are challenging; we do not get to, as the old saying goes, "throw the baby away with the bath water." There are four ways we can have relationships: We can have the wrong relationship, a partial relationship, no relationship or a godly relationship.

The wrong relationships can lead us in the wrong direction, taking us off course from the plan of God and moving us in a direction which God never intended causing our hearts to pull away from Him. The problem with moving in the wrong direction is that it sometimes takes years to reverse the direction. It causes us to lose time and even material things which God desires for us. It also can cause us to not experience the abundant life that Christ has for us here on Earth.

> The problem with moving in the wrong direction is that it sometimes takes years to reverse the direction.

Take a look at your present life. Are you where God wants you to be? Are you on God's track or your own track? Your answer to these questions is extremely important. You see "Beloved," the problem with wasted time and moving in an ungodly direction is that it might take you years to get back on the right path—if ever. Do you have any more time to waste? I know I do not, and you should not either.

In the wrong relationship, oftentimes we find ourselves taking advice from someone who has no knowledge as to where they are going, yet somehow they can see clearly where we are headed. I think this is called "the blind leading the blind."

In addition, wrong direction can lead to wrong timing in decision-making processes. God has many things for us to accomplish; however, the timing of those things is as important as the thing itself. Had Elisha missed the timing of God, he would not have received the double portion of Elijah's anointing that he requested from Elijah (2 Kings 2:9-14).

We are usually misinformed in wrong relationships opening the door to a wrong attitude toward God. Instead of allowing God to bring healing to the heart, we now make excuses, and we begin to blame others (and God) for our conditions. Without even being aware, our attitude shifts from the things of God and this causes our hearts to trust in ungodly counsel.

This is why Proverbs 4:23 tells us to "keep your heart with all diligence for out of it springs the issues of life." The healed heart understands Proverbs 4:23. It is a heart that guards itself from harm by supervising what enters in and what exits out. It is a heart that protects and shields itself from pain by not letting offenses set up roots. It is a heart that is quick to obey the Word of God allowing the Word to maintain a balance in it as different emotions are filtered.

We are all experiencing exactly what is present in our hearts even as I speak; therefore, at the end of the day, the only reflections we see in the mirror are ourselves. We should want the reflection to be positive, but that can only happen when we are honest with ourselves about all the negative hidden emotions.

Partial relationships, which are not true relationships, can also cause our hearts to be covered. This may be the most common form of relationships in the church. Let me explain what I mean by this. You and I are friends as long as I tell you what you want to hear regardless if it is right or wrong. Or better yet, I tell you part of the story, causing you to agree with me on the issues. This relationship is not real nor is it healthy.

The problem with this type of relationship is there is no integrity. It leads you to make wrong decisions because there is no truth or depth in the relationship. The relationship is superficial.

I have a friend that I am very close to, and over the years we have been very candid with one another. Some years ago I telephoned her about a major decision in my life that I had already decided. I did not need her approval, but in years past, I had always valued her opinion. I proceeded to tell her what I was planning instead of asking her to pray, and to give me her honest opinion. I remember telling her it was God, and that I knew this to be the right thing to do, not even realizing my heart was hidden and closed to the truth.

At that point, she did not try and persuade me differently because she knew I had made up my mind. What I have learned, as a pastor, is when a person tells me it is God, regardless of my thoughts (and there is a sense of assurance that the decision is not going to bring physical harm to the person or to another) I respect that person's decision.

I now know how different our relationship was compared to our present relationship. Had the relationship been truly open and honest on my part, my heart would have been open to hear what she had to say. When we have godly relationships, we may not always agree, but our hearts tend to be more open to hear what is being communicated.

Needless to say, I went ahead and did what I was planning, and she reluctantly (I found out years later) was there to support me. It was that decision that bought about the depression that I mentioned in chapter two, nearly costing me my physical life.

My point is this: I thought the relationship I had at the time with my friend was a good and open relationship. It was years later that I realized it was a partial relationship. The relationship was based on my hearing only what I wanted to hear.

We discussed the issue some years later with my apologizing for sharing only what I wanted her to know and not being honest and open enough in my heart to value her opinion. The sad thing about this decision is, it may have been the right decision, but the timing of the decision proved to be wrong.

I now advise people to wait to see consistency in behavioral changes in a person. When God has done a work in an individual, we do not have to be in a hurry. If the change is from the heart, the behavior will last putting time on our side. It is important to have people in our lives that we trust. Not to make decisions for us, but to give guidance in the decision-making process when needed.

The most dangerous of the four relationships is having no relationships at all. Adam and Eve had a wonderful relationship with God up until Eve allowed the serpent to bring deception. After which, out of fear, they hid from the presence of God removing the personal relationship they had enjoyed. Like many of us, Adam and Eve probably did not think they needed God anymore. Nothing could be further from the truth. This is when we need to call on God, and this is when He wants us to call upon Him.

A good definition for no relationship is being too busy or finding excuses for not associating with others, making oneself the soul source of one's own counsel. Nor do we speak into anyone's life; and when we do speak into someone's life our opinion always rules. We are unable and resistant to receiving advice of any kind from others.

Satan's tactic has now worked causing us to be deceived about self. We tend to believe our own views and opinions telling ourselves there is nothing wrong with us; it is others with the problems because they do not measure up to our standards. We get what I call a distorted view of self. We become self deceived and self righteous in our hearts not allowing anyone to give us advice.

We can become so deceived that our perception of others becomes distorted. We view the person through tinted glasses while looking at an early morning fog. Meaning we are not seeing clearly, or we have significant blind spots. Unfortunately, the view now becomes our reality even if it is imagined.

> We can become so deceived that our perception of others becomes distorted.

Have you ever had thoughts about a person only to find out your perceptions were wrong? The Word warns us about this in Matthew 7:1; "Judge not, that you be not judged." This behavior can easily happen when we have no relationships, and do not trust others.

Having no godly relationships is very dangerous. It can cause us to become deceived about God and His love for us. We end up hiding because we don't think we are worthy of God's love. This is a form of pride with low self-esteem. It is a pride that stands in the way when we think more highly of ourselves than we should (Romans 12:3).

We think we have all the answers to life's problems, and this must be true because we look successful. We live in the right neighborhoods, drive the right cars, and we know the right people. 2 Timothy 3:5 says, "having a form of godliness but denying its power;" looks can be deceiving. How many times has a particular food looked good to eat, only to find that what we ate was not good for us? Oh my, this sounds like the Garden of Eden!

Now the deception stops our spiritual and emotional growth and causes us to function out of this distorted view of self which is emotionally unhealthy. At this point, it is hard to change, so we remain in the same place emotionally year after year.

Do not be fooled as Eve was, over 4,000 years ago. Know that the same devil who deceived Eve "walks about like a roaring lion, seeking whom he may devour" (1 Peter 5:8). Do not open the door to the enemy of our soul, satan, with an attitude that says "I don't need anyone." Remember it was God that instituted relationships; therefore, it must be important to Him, and He wants us to have godly relationships that provoke us to be more Christ-like.

He is a God that loved His creation so much that He sent Jesus to die so that we might be restored to Him. This is what righteousness is all about. Even when we miss it, we are still righteous because our righteousness has nothing to do with us. We are declared righteous because of the blood of Christ. Our hearts are now complete in Him forever. There is nothing we can do and nothing more we need to do.

Romans 5:8-11 says it like this:

But God demonstrates His own love toward us, in that while we were still sinners, Christ died for us. Much more then, having now been justified by His blood, we shall be saved from wrath through Him. For if when we were enemies we were reconciled to God through the death of His Son, much more, having been reconciled, we shall be saved by His life. And not only that, but we also rejoice in God through our Lord Jesus Christ, through whom we have now received the reconciliation.

The last relationship is a right godly relationship—a relationship built on trusting God and trusting one another. However, we must trust God first. When we trust someone, we believe what they say without argument or doubt. I like how the Apostle James talks about trust when he speaks about faith in James 1:5-6; "If any of you lacks wisdom, let him ask of God, who gives to all liberally and without reproach, and it will be given to him. But let him ask in faith, with no doubting, for he who doubts is like a wave of the sea driven and tossed by the wind."

> When we trust someone, we believe what they say without argument or doubt.

There is no room for doubting when we read this scripture. You either trust God or you don't. If we knew that every decision we made relied on our trust in others, we probably would be more open and understanding in our hearts when it comes to trusting them. We would be less likely to judge a person if we knew our very life depended on that trust.

Well, this is the case with God; our very life depends on our trust in Him. He is the only one who will never disappoint us. He is the one who is always there when everyone else is gone. He is the one who took our heart and turned it into a heart of flesh so we could fellowship with Him when and wherever we want.

Let us look at how the healed heart responds when we have right godly relationships, and what these relationships bring to our lives. In your personal study time, read 2 King 2:9-12; it is about Elijah and Elisha who had a father and son relationship even though Elijah was not Elisha's birth father.

Prior to Elijah being taken by God, Elisha made a decision wherever Elijah went he would go; Elisha decided he was not going to leave the man of God. Three times Elijah instructed Elisha to stay put while he went and took care of the Lord's business, but Elisha said no.

It is significant that Elisha was told three times to remain and three times he did not for the number three means solid, real, complete and entire. It denotes divine perfection, Father, Son and Holy Spirit, and it also denotes the sum of human capability, thought, word and deed. Elisha was faithful in all three human capabilities. He thought through his decisions, he spoke his decisions, and he followed his decisions. He was committed to serving the man of God.

Because of Elisha's heart, Elijah asked what he could do for him, and Elisha replied. "Please let a double portion of your spirit be upon me" (2 Kings 2:9). Elisha was told what would happen if he saw his master taken, and that is exactly what happened.

Elisha received a double portion.

The double portion was not just the anointing; Elisha also received growth and promotion far beyond his mentor. He was immediately respected by the prophets, and they bowed before him. Elisha's promotion was a result of a godly relationship. The promotion was so profound that Elisha went on to do greater things in God than Elijah. Elijah's miracles were eight in number. Elisha's miracles were sixteen in number, and after Elisha died, a dead man touched his bones and lived. "A man was put in the tomb of Elisha; and when the man was let down and touched the bones of Elisha, he revived and stood on his feet" (2 Kings 13:21). This is the power of godly relationships.

We must understand that we are not in this fight alone, and yes, it is a battle but we know the end results—we win. Letting go of the past and trusting others is a step of faith we must take if we want our hearts to be healed.

Do not allow the enemy of your soul (satan) to stop you from finding true godly relationships. Your life will be better for it as you give and receive what God has for you through others.

6

The Renewed Heart

When you do not know who you are in Christ, or what the Word of God says about who you are in Him, your heart can become full of doubt and unbelief. In order to operate from the renewed heart you must know who you are in Christ and what your identity is in Him. This knowing produces good self-esteem. Within this good self-esteem, two basic needs are important in order to function as God intended. These needs are acceptance and identity.

It is normal to want to be accepted. This is how I believe God made us. However, when we have a need to be accepted by everyone, we start to allow our emotions to rule our hearts and control our behavior. At some time or another, we all have tried to fit in with our peers. Maybe it was at work, school, church, or even within our own families.

For example, have you ever experienced being in a conversation with a group of people, and you felt as though you had nothing to contribute, but you desperately wanted to be included in the conversation? You felt left out regardless of what you did or said. This could be an unhealthy need to be accepted.

Christ was not accepted; therefore, we need to put acceptance into its proper perspective in order to avoid being trapped in a cycle of trying to get everyone to accept us. There is a difference between the basic need of acceptance and a neediness to be accepted by others.

The neediness to be accepted places us in a condition in which there is a deficiency of something emotional in our souls—a state of extreme want feeding our emotions. This deficiency in our emotions can only be filled by God. We are already accepted, "To the praise of the glory of His grace, by which He made us accepted in the Beloved" (Ephesians 1:6). This means we do not have to strive to be accepted by others for Christ has already made us acceptable, lovely and deserving of love.

To take it a step further, Christ not only has accepted us, He also chose us as His very own. "Blessed be the God and Father of our Lord Jesus Christ, who has blessed us with every spiritual blessing in the heavenly places in Christ, just as He chose us in Him before the foundation of the world, that we should be holy and without blame before Him in love" (Ephesians 1:3-4). We are selected and chosen to Christ Himself, establishing a relationship, and giving us favor as a chosen vessel of God.

Isn't that wonderful? You were chosen by God. Know that it is okay when we are not accepted by others because we are always accepted by God, and in His acceptance He never places demands upon us. Yes, He desires for us to change and grow, but His acceptance of us is not based on that change. It is based on His

Son's righteousness. When we came to Christ and received Him as Savior and Lord His acceptance of us became permanent. I thank God that Christ already paid the price for my image.

"What then shall we say to these things? If God is for us, who can be against us?" (Romans 8:31). The Word *for* here means God is exceedingly, abundantly, beyond or over the top for us. God is so far

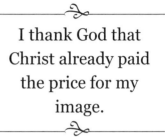

I thank God that Christ already paid the price for my image.

over the top for us that He comes to our defense. His Word is telling us that nothing will come against us that He cannot handle on our behalf.

However, we tend to really struggle in this area. Yes, it is a basic need to be accepted, but who accepts us is the question. Is it important that every person we meet accept us? No, it is not important, nor is it possible.

It took me many years to come to the understanding that everyone was not going to like me, and I had to make a decision that the behavior of others would not affect who I was, or how I performed.

This is an important point. We must come to the place that being accepted by others does not dictate our behavior. However, we cannot come to this place in our hearts if we do not know who we are in Christ.

"For whom He foreknew, He also predestined to be conformed to the image of His Son, that He might be the firstborn among many brethren" (Romans 8:29). God knew you beforehand and has a plan for you. The plan God has for you, He created before the foundation of the world, giving you the very image of His Son,

Jesus Christ. Jesus is the firstborn among many brethren; you are one of the many brethren! "Moreover whom he predestined, these He also called; who He called, these He also justified; and whom He justified, these He also glorified" (Romans 8:30).

This is awesome! God not only made us to look like Him, but He made us to act like Him, and He gave us Grace, which is His ability in us to help us to be like Him. We are justified (acquitted) by faith in Jesus Christ, declared righteous by a Holy God, and bought to honor by Jesus' death, burial and resurrection.

We are molded into the image of Christ as His "Beloved." This is how we should identify ourselves. Man's identity of us should not carry any weight, nor should we emotionally be bound to other's acceptance of us.

There are people whose acceptance of us is a normal expectation. For me, it is my family and some personal friends. But this does not mean they should agree with everything I do or say. I am sure there are others who accept me; however, that acceptance should not dictate my behavior. My behavior should be Christ-like regardless.

Jesus recognized this in His ministry. "So they were offended at Him. But Jesus said to them, a prophet is not without honor except in his own country and in his own house. Now He did not do many mighty works there because of their unbelief" (Matthew 13:57-58). Jesus obviously was not accepted not only in his hometown, but He was not received as the Savior by His own: "He came to His own, and His own did not receive Him" (John 1:11).

Even as born again believers, we have operated out of codependent behavior knowingly and unknowingly. It takes a conscious decision to change this kind of behavior. Some years ago, I spoke at a women's fellowship about these issues. I remember telling the ladies that I make decisions based on whether that decision is good for my family even if the decision causes people not to accept me. This included decisions I would make on my job. You probably are thinking: "most of us make decisions in the same manner." Not so. Most of us make decisions based on being accepted.

We are to be led by the Holy Spirit in our decision-making processes. However, when we are not sure of our identity in Christ, we let the flesh, our ability, dominate and rule. We live our lives on a roller coaster, or better yet, we live life like a hamster.

Have you ever watched a hamster in a cage? The hamster eats, sleeps, poops and rides the wheel in the cage over and over.

This is what happens to us when we fail to recognize who we are in Christ. Life becomes a circle of cycles. We keep going through the same cycles over and over.

If you think I am wrong, stop right now and look back over your life the last 20 years. Write down the patterns in your life and see if much has changed. If not, you are reliving a circle of cycles like the hamster. You are constantly going around and around looking for things to change, yet continuing to do the same old things.

We have been handpicked by God, and it is His will that we accomplish all that He has predestined. I would encourage you to meditate on Ephesians 1:3-14. You are the "Beloved," and no one else will ever love you like Jesus. He will never leave you nor will He every disappoint you. Yes, we love one another, but more than not, we love with conditions attached. Christ's love has no conditions attached and His love never ends.

The awesome part about God's acceptance is that there is nothing we can do to make ourselves more acceptable. We

Christ's love has no conditions attached and His love never ends.

were so ugly, filthy and dirty that it took Jesus going to the Cross to make us amiable. The Cross is a complete work. When God looks at us, He only sees His Son. What is important for us to do is receive Jesus' acceptance of us, and not look to anyone else for validation; our validation can only come from Christ.

Your identity is directly tied to receiving God's love for you. Jesus died for the world. "For God so loved the world that He gave His only begotten Son, that whosoever believes in Him should not perish but have everlasting life" (John 3:16).

Although we did not deserve it, God's love caused Him to give His very best. Those of us who have received Christ as our personal Savior are commanded to allow God's Grace (His ability in us) to transform our minds. We are to be changed from the inside out.

When we get saved, the only One who can see the immediate change is God because change is a condition of the heart. It is not until we allow the Word of God to change us in our souls that others can see the inward change which is reflected on the outside.

The born again experience is a change in our spirit. The soul is saved which stops us from going to hell; however, the three parts of the soul (mind, will, and emotions) must be dealt with through the Word of God.

The mind is the real issue we must deal with. Strong's New

Testament Complete Word Study defines the mind as the organ of mental perceptions and apprehension, the organ of conscious life; the organ of the consciousness preceding actions or recognizing and judging actions. The mind functions through the heart. This is why it so important for our perceptions to be God-centered and not self-centered.

The mind that is self-centered is what Paul talks about in the book of Romans, the carnal mind. The carnal mind only thinks about self's views, ideas, and opinions. This self-centeredness is the root of most of the problems both believers and non-believers experience.

We are not to give into self, and we have the Spirit of the living God on the inside of us giving the power not to surrender to our flesh. Paul tells us, "I beseech you therefore, brethren, by the mercies of God, that you present your bodies a living sacrifice, holy acceptable to God, which is your reasonable service, and do not be conformed to this world, but be transformed by the renewing of your mind, that you may prove what is that good and acceptable and perfect will of God" (Romans 12:1-2).

We need to get a clear understanding of what God is commanding us to do in this scripture. When a child is dedicated to the Lord it is a serious matter. The parents are saying the child will be raised to walk along side of the Lord, placing the care of the child in the Lord's hands.

This is what we are to do with our bodies. We are to walk along side with the Lord, and we are to be set apart in our bodies as a living sacrifice acceptable and well pleasing in worship to God.

We are to have no attachment to the things in the world, and we are to allow deep change in our souls (mind, will, emotions) qualitatively. We are to be transformed, which means a change of condition or different physical form. This qualitative transformation comes through the process of renewing or renovating our mental perceptions and apprehensions.

Have you every renovated a room in your home? Renewing the mind is the same process. When you began the process, you needed certain materials, tools, paint, wall paper, etc. What you need to renovate your conscious perceptions is the Word of God.

You must understand your spirit is perfect, but your mind, which is a part of your soul that operates through your heart, must be renewed. When you begin to renovate your conscious perceptions with the Word of God through daily reading, praying, and meditating on the Word, you will experience a profound change in your thought patterns.

Your soul, which is separate from your spirit, will begin to move closer and closer to your spirit. Let me do a demonstration with you. Put both your hands in front of you with a gap between the two facing each other. The left hand is your spirit and the right hand is your soul. Slowly begin to move your right hand toward the left hand...

As you do this, think about your soul moving closer to your spirit day by day to where there is hardly any gap between the two. We know that perfection will totally come when Christ returns; however, I am convinced we can and should be living the abundant life that Christ talks about.

It is sad to see born again, spirit-filled Christians who have sat in church for years, but have not experienced a true transformation in their minds. They still experience the negative emotions we talked about in chapter two, even though the Word of God is available to bring about permanent change. This change causes us to discern what is profitable and useful, and it is this change that brings us to maturity in Christ not morally lacking in our perceptions. The type of transformation I am speaking of is not just for preachers. It is available for all who believe, "For there is no partiality with God" (Romans 2:11).

The renewing of your mind is hard work and requires consistency.

> *But be doers of the word, and not hearers only, deceiving yourselves. For if anyone is a hearer of the word and not a doer, he is like a man observing his natural face in a mirror; for he observes himself, goes away, and immediately forgets what kind of man he was. But he who looks into the perfect law of liberty and continues in it, and is not a forgetful hearer, but a doer of the word, this one will be blessed in what he does* (James 1:22-25).

There is nothing worse than deceiving yourself, which means you are being a fool to yourself. If you read the Word, quote the Word, pray the Word, but never do the Word, what was the point? "Faith without works is dead" (James 2:20).

The man in the mirror in James 1:23 gained nothing as far as the real purpose and power of God is concerned. Sure he could say, "I hear the Word," but walking away with no corresponding action meant that was all he could say. He did not put the Word into action, and although he had awareness, he even lost that, as the Word dropped out of his mind.

Unfortunately, we all have been guilty of this very thing. We continue to hear the Word of God over and over again with no application of the Word. This means the Word is awareness only. I believe that had the man in James 1:23 continued and also acted on the Word, he would not have been a forgetful hearer. Unlike this man, I want my life to change daily more into the image of Christ. Can you say the same? If so, welcome to a renewed life in Christ!

This change will not be a one-time changing. We are to be transformed in our mental perceptions or conscious life that precedes our actions daily. Our thinking and our knowing becomes transformed as we take out the old and put in the new. We no longer will think, judge, perceive or act from the old man, our perceptions are now new, our judgment is now new, our understanding is now new. We will begin to pay attention to the things of the spirit and not the things of the flesh (our abilities).

My husband and I were recently discussing personal change. What we know to be true is people will only change when they make a decision to do so, but what we don't understand is that we are changing daily regardless, even when we do not make the decision to change.

You see, Beloved, we are always changing. The question is, how and in what way are we changing? If we do not make a conscious decision to emotionally change and move forward, the unconscious decision is causing us to move backward. We are never standing still, we are either moving forward or backward.

We change our minds everyday in some way or another. I remember when I was planning our wedding; I changed my mind many times about the colors for the wedding. Not because

I did not know what color I wanted, it was because I was looking for the right dress which was more important to me than the color. Well this is not a problem for Jesus; He is always dressed appropriately, and He will dress you appropriately from head to toe if you allow Him.

We all must choose to make changes in our hearts, for the time is short for all of us. The young have no more time than the old because time is the same for each of us—God does not favor one over the other. God's desire is for us to change more into the image of His Son. He made us to live the abundant life here on earth; therefore, we must open our hearts to receive change; for it is good for the soul!

7

The Changed Heart

I believe God desires for our character to reflect Him in all that we do and say. In Luke 23:47 after Christ died it reads, "And when the centurion saw what had happened, he glorified God, saying, 'Certainly this was a righteous man!'" Can someone look at you and say the same?

You see "Beloved," after we have moved and flowed in the gifts of the Spirit which is given by the Spirit as He wills (1 Corinthians 12:11), all that is left is our character. We should not live out of the gifts alone; we should live out of the character of Christ which should be a direct reflection of what is in our heart.

Our spirit man is born again and we now have the nature of Christ on the inside; however, we must do something about those areas in our hearts that are not like Christ. King David said in Psalms 51:10, "Create in me a clean heart, O God, and renew a steadfast spirit within me."

Luke 24:32 says, "did not our heart (thoughts, passions,

desires, appetites, affections, purposes, endeavors), burn within us while He (Jesus) talked with us on the road, and while He opened the Scriptures to us?" (Emphasis added). The disciples knew that a change had occurred within their hearts.

This is important to understand because your heart is who you are, good, bad or indifferent, and you always communicate out of your heart. Recently, we were having Bible study when I asked the question—what about nonverbal communication? We speak in many different ways. In fact, my husband recently taught that everything has a voice.

He used the scripture in which Jesus cursed the fig tree. "And seeing from afar a fig tree having leaves, He went to see if perhaps He would find something on it. When He came to it, He found nothing but leaves, for it was not the season for figs. In response Jesus said to it..." In response to what? In response to the fig tree—the tree had a voice. It was speaking to Jesus; therefore, Jesus responded by saying "Let no one eat fruit from you ever again" (Mark 11:13-14).

We all know that the tree did not audibly speak to Jesus, yet its voice caused Jesus to respond to nonverbal communication. Our actions say volumes. I remember when I was a child, my mother only had to look at me and my siblings in church, and we would immediately stop whatever we were doing. She never spoke a word; she would just look.

If we say one thing and then do something totally different from what we say, that is a problem, and the problem rests in our heart. This is what James talks about when he speaks of being double minded. Although we may be trying to hide, our heart gives us away; it locates us.

God is after this change of heart first and foremost. I once heard a minister say a baby can operate in the gifts; however, a change in the heart, which can change our character, requires willingness from the heart with a dependence on the ability of God who rests inside us.

The heart is, and always will be, how God communicates with us. Man's heart was so important to God that He destroyed the earth with the flood because of the wickedness in man's heart. "Then the Lord saw that the wickedness of man was great in the earth, and that every intent of the thoughts of his heart was only evil continually" (Gen. 6:5). We can see here our hearts do talk, and we naturally follow what the heart is saying.

We follow our hearts through emotions of our wills. Whatever it is that you are doing, you first conceived it in your heart, and then you birthed it through your actions willfully. Numbers 15:39b tells us that "we follow the harlotry to which our own hearts and our own eyes are inclined if we do not remember all God's commandments" (emphasis added).

It is clear that the people during Noah's day followed after fleshly desires, and God said "He was sorry that He had made man on the earth, and He was grieved in His heart" (Genesis. 6:6). God was not merely upset; God felt great sorrow in His heart for having made man. The sorrow was so great that verse seven tells us, "I will destroy man who I have created from the face of the earth, both man and beast, creeping thing and birds of the air, for I am sorry that I have made them" (Gen. 6:7).

Yet, even in God's sorrow, He had mercy on man, for "Noah found grace in the eyes of the Lord" (Genesis. 6:8). As wicked as man was and still is today, the Lord has not given up on His most prized creation. Through the power of the Holy Spirit, God still continues to draw men to repentance giving us an opportunity to no longer allow our hearts to "follow the harlotry to which our hearts and our own eyes are inclined" to rule (Numbers 15:39b).

The change that God is seeking in our heart is the change that reflects an unequivocally distinguishable difference in our character between us and the world. When the world sees us, they should see a reflection of our heavenly Father in our behavior and emotions.

I am reminded of Jabez, whose name meant he will cause pain. Every time Jabez heard his name as a child, this is what was being spoken. At some point in Jabez's life, "Jabez called on the God of Israel saying, oh, that you would bless me indeed, and enlarge my territory, that Your hand would be with me, and that You would keep me from evil, that I may not cause pain, so God granted him what he requested" (1 Chronicles 4:10).

Little is known about Jabez, but in my studying, I found that Jabez's linage is from the tribe of Judah; the same linage as Christ Himself. Like Christ, regardless of what was said about him, Jabez was destined to be great, but that greatness would only be fulfilled with the right heart.

In his heart, he chose not to wear his name as a banner of defeat; instead, he called upon the God of Israel despite what his name said about him. Jabez did not let what he heard rule his heart. He knew that God had the final word about who he was, and it was that knowing that kept his heart and gave him peace.

The changed heart will always reflect peace. It is frustrating to desire the peace of God, but not know how to seek and rest in the peace of God. Isaiah 26:3 gives us a clear view of the process of God's peace. "You (God) will keep him (us) in perfect peace, whose mind is stayed on You (Him), because he (we) trust in You (Him)" (emphasis added). This is a promise from God that He will guard, protect, watch, and preserve us in perfect peace when our mind remains focused on Him.

The peace that God is speaking about means He will cause us to be safe, whole, and secure in Him. However, there are some conditions to this promise, and the conditions cause us to look at our hearts. The second part of verse three says, "whose mind is stayed on You, because he trusts in You."

When we are troubled in our hearts, the thoughts we have are not always on God or the things of God. We tend to let our minds wander, focusing on the negative issues that occur in our lives. What we must begin to do is pattern our imaginations or thoughts after the Word of God.

Again, Philippians 4:8 tells us, "whatever things are true, whatever things are noble, whatever things are just, whatever things are pure, whatever things are of a good report, if there is any virtue and if there is anything praiseworthy, meditate on these things."

Make a decision to meditate on the Word of God. Doing so will be life changing in your heart, reflecting God's goodness, faithfulness, mercy and grace on the outside.

Keep your mind fixed and established on Christ with confidence that you can trust Him. Oh!! The peace of God, what joy it brings us to know that we can rely on a God who loves us and is concerned about every intricate detail of our lives. Hebrews 4:15a tells us "For we do not have a High Priest who cannot sympathize with our weaknesses." I don't know about you, but I find this to be awesome!

No one else cares or thinks about me in this manner. Years ago, I remember driving to work one morning thinking about the goodness of God, and how He loved me even knowing every sin I would commit beforehand.

I was so over taken with the peace of God that morning, I began to weep and praise the Lord. Upon arriving to work my eyes were puffy, and most of my make up was gone, but it did not matter because I finally realized just how awesome God's love is toward me, and His peace rested deep in my heart bringing a change in my soul.

Let your heart be transformed by the Word of God. Make a decision today to consistently pray the Word, study the Word, and meditate on the Word. There is no formula, but if you just need one, this would be it. Praying, studying, and meditating on the Word of God will cause your heart to follow after your Maker, and in that process, it will change you and how you view everything around you.

8

The Mature Heart

I can remember when I was a teenager how I wanted to be thought of as being "grown up." I wanted to be treated as an adult even though I was not an adult. My mother would say "stop trying to be grown—it will happen soon enough." And it did. We know growing up is more than a change in age, it is also maturing and accepting responsibility for our actions. Well it is similar in spiritual maturity. The goal is not simply to flow in the gifts—the goal is to mature in Christ in our thoughts and actions.

As I share with others, I am constantly reminded to tell them how God is always working on maturing us in our character.

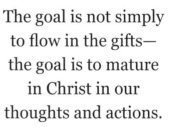

The goal is not simply to flow in the gifts— the goal is to mature in Christ in our thoughts and actions.

Since instability and immaturity go together, it is important to be stable in all areas of life. When we are spiritually mature,

97

the heart will function as God designed. This is the heart that recognizes issues in life come and go and these issues should be used to strengthen us in our minds and our characters. Unfortunately, many of us live year after year with a broken heart not allowing the maturity of Christ to manifest. This lack of maturity in the heart can be directly reflective of a broken heart.

When we speak of a broken heart, we are sometimes reminded of romantically being broken-hearted. In this instance, we usually see ourselves as being mistreated or perhaps ditched for someone else and we are left with this broken heart. It is this heart which believes and feels justified to hide because of disappointment and/or rejection from those we believed loved us. We close off our hearts, we make the determination that there is no need or room for openness—besides it was openness that caused the vulnerability in the first place, right? Regardless of the reason, a broken heart is a very serious matter. Psalm 69:20 gives us the depth of a broken heart; "Reproach has broken my heart, and I am full of heaviness; I looked for someone to take pity, but there was none; and for comforters, but I found none."

Reproach causes the heart to feel lack of self worth, ashamed, disgraced, or even condemned. The word *broken* in this context means *shattered*, and this shattering causes the heart to become heavy or weighted down. It also means there is a sadness deep within our soul (mind, will, emotions) when we are broken-hearted making it difficult to find comfort. This is the heart that easily falls into loneliness (and often chooses loneliness) because of the pain it believes it has suffered.

When the heart is broken, we feel as though it has burst open or been broken into a million pieces. The physical heart is an organ in our body which is about the size of a fist. If it were shattered into a million pieces, it would no longer function—simply put, we would physically die. It is the same with an emotionally broken heart. We no longer function in the manner God designed in our mind, will and emotions. Just like the physical heart shuts down if shattered in a million pieces, so will the new heart God speaks about in Ezekiel 36:26; "I will give you a new heart and put a new spirit within you; I will take the heart of stone out of your flesh and give you a heart of flesh."

There are many things that can cause the heart to be broken; however, we will focus on two; the first being rejection and the second disappointments. Jesus Himself experienced immense rejection. Isaiah 53:3 says "He is despised and rejected by men, A man of sorrows and acquainted with grief. And we hid, as it were, our faces from Him; He was despised and we did not esteem Him."

This Scripture gives a clear picture of what it means to be rejected by someone. We feel as though we have been thrown away, forsaken, or discarded and worthless. This is exactly how Jesus must have felt during His earthly ministry. His own people refused to accept Him which brought not only rejection, but also humiliation. Yet, 2 Corinthians 5:21 tells us, "For He made Him who knew no sin to be sin for us, that we might become the righteousness of God in Him." Because of righteousness, we do not have to allow the spirit of rejection to operate in our lives.

Once rejection sets up residence in our souls, our personal actions and reactions to the issues of life become clouded and distorted. We tend to twist things around to justify feeling the way we do or we may even try and hide our true feelings giving a false sense of security. When we act and react negatively to situations in our life from rejection, we usually have a strong need to be accepted. Although we may not communicate openly verbally, we may find ourselves needing to be around people all the time in order to feel secure. Unfortunately, if left to fester in our hearts, rejection is a negative emotion we can struggle with for many years, if not the remainder of our lives. The struggle not only appears in our neediness to be accepted, it can also be seen in our attempt to control and manipulate those around us.

Over the years, I have observed that when we struggle with rejection, if we are not included, often times we will twist and misrepresent issues to be seen and heard. Not even realizing how inappropriate our behavior has become, we often turn simple things into major catastrophes. The root cause of rejection is fear. Fear of being rejected all over again. Fear of not being loved. Fear of not be accepted. Fear of being alone...fear of everything! In order to nullify this fear, we must begin with forgiveness. This is where we must start when struggling with rejection. Forgiveness is the key that unlocks the door to a broken heart, helping the heart to mature.

> Forgiveness is the key that unlocks the door to a broken heart, helping the heart to mature.

The rejected and immature heart often times brings out emotional insecurities. When we are insecure we tend to worry about everything. We worry about how we look, how we sound, how we are viewed by others—everything! The problem with this is worry leads to anxiousness and apprehension. When we need to make a rational decision, the process is hindered by our own insecurities. I continue to learn that very few decisions require the amount of energy and time that we use. "Don't sweat the small stuff" is real because 98% of what we experience is small stuff. Can we save the drama for the remaining 2%?

We do not hear this preached enough, but worry is sin. Jesus tells us in Matthew 6:25, "Therefore I say to you, do not worry about your life, what you will eat or what you will drink; nor about your body, what you will put on. Is not life more than food and the body more than clothing?" Do not let the issues of life trouble you causing you to be fearful sinking your heart into despair. With life come tests, trials, and temptations for all of us. None of us are excluded, yet how we handle these issues is what I believe to be the difference between living the abundant life Jesus speaks about in John chapter ten, or living a life of quiet desperation.

It is a terrible thing to be insecure in your emotions—emotionally unable to make a decision for fear of making the wrong decision. I remember years ago having an intern who worked for me. As bright and intelligent as she was, she struggled with making decisions. She needed approval from those in authority or she was paralyzed when it came to making decisions. Because I try not to micro manage in leading others this became even more of a problem for her. Finally, my assistant at the time told her if she wanted to please me, she should "make a decision." Even if it was the wrong decision, it is was better than not making a decision at all. The advice given to her was good, but she still struggled because of her fear of rejection in her soul that caused the insecurity.

It is important for us to understand that our security rests in the finished work of Christ. There is nothing that He did not take for us in His death. Isaiah 53:4–5 tells us, "Surely He has borne our griefs And carried our sorrows; Yet we esteemed Him stricken, Smitten by God, and afflicted. But He was wounded for our transgressions, He was bruised for our iniquities; The chastisement for our peace was upon Him, And by His stripes we are healed." "Beloved" let me describe what Christ did on the cross for you and me.

Isaiah 53 4–5 paraphrased by Helen:

Certainly, He has lifted; taken away my sickness and my diseases, and my anxieties, and my calamities, and He carried away my pain. He was stained, defiled, polluted for my rebellion and, my sins. He was beat to pieces, crushed, oppressed, humbled, and destroyed for my faults. The discipline, correction, rebuke, punishment for my well being, for my health, for my safety, for my wholeness was upon, against, was charged to Him. And by His black and blue marks on His body, by His bruises, by His hurts, by His wounds, by His bounding with stripes I am cured, I am repaired, I am healed, I am thoroughly made whole.

These Scriptures tell us we have been redeemed and delivered from insecurities, fears, anxiousness, worries, apprehensions, uncertainty, troubles and any other emotion or mental state that stops us from being who we are in Christ. Because of His deliverance, we do not and should not let a broken heart with all its entrapments dictate the circumstances of our lives. Have you ever asked someone how they were doing—with their response being, "...under the circumstances"? "Beloved," what are you doing under the circumstances? When

> When I read Isaiah 53, all my circumstances are under the blood of Christ.

I read Isaiah 53, all my circumstances are under the blood of Christ.

Understand, although Jesus has taken all on the Cross for us does not mean that we will not have adversities. We will have adversities as long as the enemy of our soul, satan, remains loosed on this earth; however, Isaiah 53 tells me there is nothing left for me to carry. Jesus has taken away all my grief, all my anxieties, all my calamities, all my sickness, all my pain (mentally, physically, emotionally) and all my sorrows. When I carry any of these issues that happen in my life, I am making a conscious decision to do so. I recognize that this is not easy, but 2 Corinthians 5:7 says, "For we walk by faith (belief and unwavering trust in God whether we see anything or not) and not by sight" (Emphasis added by author).

It is now time to allow the Word of God to bring healing to your broken heart so that you can perform up to your God given capabilities with the mature heart He has supplied. You are not only capable of so much more—you deserve so much more!!!

However, it is not enough just to speak this only—we must begin to live it right now! Living it starts with loving ourselves. Over the years, I have heard different schools of thought about self love. Some believe that loving oneself is arrogant and leads to selfishness. I believe, however, that it is impossible to love another without first loving self. Matthew 19:18b says, "You shall love your neighbor as yourself." How can we extend love to another if we cannot extend love to ourselves?

> How can we extend love to another if we cannot extend love to ourselves?

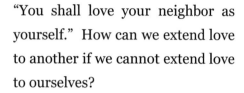

True love of self will not allow a broken heart to consume its soul (mind, will, emotions). It will allow the mature heart to control and direct its mind, will and emotions. When a broken heart consumes the soul we shut down and become passive, receiving but not acting, in our soul. What do I mean by "not acting?" We stop trusting others, because the heart is so hidden it does not respond to others trying to enter. I believe we subconsciously make decisions to shut others out by building walls around our hearts helping to hide them.

Unlike the wounded heart, which responds out of its wounds (past hurts), the broken heart tends not to respond at all. Can you remember your first real crush or what you thought was love at the time? When you realized the person you had the crush on did not feel the same way, how did you react? I remember what I did—I literally shut down. I did not want to see anyone nor did I want to talk to anyone. I now know that most of what I was experiencing was embarrassment, but you get my point.

Unfortunately, when we experience being broken hearted as an adult, it can be debilitating causing us to become physically inactive, lifeless, unenthusiastic and unresponsive. It is very easy at this point for depression to take control of our lives. We must guard against this with the Word of God by planting the Word of God in our hearts, through study, meditation, and prayer. I am convinced that the Word of God is what saved my life in 1995. It was not just the casually read Word; it was the in-depth Word that I had studied and meditated on for years prior—the Word that was hidden in my heart.

You see "Beloved," we cannot jump into the Word of God, and expect instant results when we have not had a lifestyle of daily studying and meditating on the Word. This is what my husband calls a 911 relationship with God. We only call upon Him when we have an emergency. Where is the maturity in that? Test and trails are a part of life—they will always present themselves. We must come to understand that the Word of God *must be* a daily "way of life;" then tests and trails become no match for the Word. The Word that has been sown in your heart year after year will rise and empower you not only to face life's challenges head on, but to overcome them.

One form of broken heartedness is disappointment. Disappointments come when we or others fall short of expected results. This type of broken heart brings frustration, regret, disillusion, and discouragement causing us to experience trouble in our souls and setbacks in our lives.

Have you ever been so frustrated that nothing seems to happen? If so, this is exactly what is supposed to occur. When we are frustrated everything becomes nullified. Frustration works similarly to fear. With fear we become paralyzed and when we are frustrated those things we want to see changed become paralyzed as a result of our frustration. Nothing seems to work even though, unlike being paralyzed with fear, we are still trying to make things happen. I remember years ago helping one of my children with a homework assignment. The longer I worked with her the more frustrated I became, yet I continued to try and help even though there was no results. This is what occurs when we are frustrated—we keep trying but the results are blocked.

Another word for frustration is deception. When we read Genesis chapter three, which talks about the temptation and fall of man, we can see that Eve was deceived:

> *Now the serpent was more cunning than any beast of the field which the Lord God had made. And he said to the woman. "Has God indeed said, 'You shall not eat of every tree of the garden'?" And the woman said to the serpent, "We may eat the fruit of the trees of the garden; "but of the fruit of the tree which is in the midst of the garden, God has said, 'You shall not eat it, nor shall you touch it, lest you die.'" Then the serpent said to the woman, "You will not surely die. "For God knows that in the day you eat of it your eyes will be opened, and you will be like God, knowing good and evil." So when the woman saw that the tree was good for food, that it was pleasant to the eyes, and a tree desirable to make one wise, she took of its fruit and ate. She also gave to her husband with her, and he ate* (Genesis 3:1–6).

Sometimes we open the door to disappointments in our lives. Eve saw that the tree was good for food. Everything that looks good is not necessarily good for us. This must have been "one heck of a piece of fruit" because it caused the first woman to disregard what God had spoken. When I was a teenager, I can remember hearing and also saying "looks are everything." I now know that looks, if not discerned properly, can bring death. However, it was not looks alone that caused Eve to eat the fruit; she also was deceived into believing she was lacking something

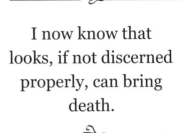

I now know that looks, if not discerned properly, can bring death.

in her life. How sad is this? Here Eve had everything—she was made perfect with nothing missing and nothing broken and she still yielded to temptation.

Unfortunately, this is us also. We have been given a new heart and the Word of God to show us how to operate with this new heart, yet somehow we think we are lacking something. So we go through life with a heart that has been broken into a million pieces when all we need to do is draw on the reservoir of life (Jesus) that is on the inside of us. This reservoir is the source of all life. It is even the source of life for those who are not born again and unknowingly searching for that reservoir every day.

What caused Eve to have a conversation with the serpent? Up until this point scripturally, we only see Adam and Eve communicating with God for sure and undoubtedly with one another. Now satan appears and disguises himself as a serpent or a snake that can talk. The Scripture does not show any concern on Eve's part that this particular creature could speak, so she proceeded to have a conversation with him. Remember Eve only knew "good" at this point. She knew no evil; however, her innocence led to the willful disobedience that brought about the fall of mankind.

We must not let frustrations cause us to be deceived as Eve. Since frustration tricks us, brings deception or nullifies our good intentions, we must turn the table in our broken hearts and bring frustration to naught in our lives. Bring it to nothingness...bring it to a place where it has no control in our souls. I have learned that peace and frustration will not reside in the heart simultaneously. When I am peaceful, there is no frustration; and when I am frustrated, there is no peace.

Disappointments bring no peace and no peace leads to discouragement. Simply put, discouragement is the absence of courage in our lives. It is a draining negative emotion causing us to lack the courage to do the things that we know we have been called by God to do. When I think about discouragement, it makes me feel as though life itself is being sucked out of me. I feel as though there is nothing left on the inside and all my strength is gone. This is significant because when we do not have strength, it is difficult to move forward. We become bankrupt in our desires and our wills.

This type of heart causes us to be and feel remorseful over things that have occurred in our lives; especially those things left unfinished. Our feelings usually directly relate to unfinished relationships and the unfinished plans that were connected to those relationships. Failure and lack of emotional strength sets in, adding to our already low self esteem, and we allow the lack of strength to bring feelings of regret. The saddest thing about regret is how it sets us back in life.

Over the last few years, I have observed born again believers live a life of constant setbacks or interruptions in progress. They move forward a little and then they are hampered. Why is this?

I believe it is a direct result of not being willing to admit where we are in our hearts, thus holding up our own progress in God. It is easy to blame someone else for our lack of progress, but if we are honest with ourselves, we will truly say where the problem lies—in us.

In our sanctuary we have a sign that says "Way of Life Forward in Faith." This is to remind us not to let rejection and disappointment rob us of what God has said and to stay focused on what He wants us to do. Yes, it can be disheartening when others disappoint us, but we do not have to let discouragement deprive us of our confidence in Christ or our confidence in what He has said about us. Isaiah 54:17: " 'No weapon formed against you shall prosper, and every tongue which rises against you in judgment You shall condemn. This is the heritage of the servants of the Lord, and their righteousness is from Me,' says the Lord." I strongly recommend meditating on this Scripture for God has said that this Word is our heritage to those of us that are His servants.

You know the amazing thing about a broken heart is that it can be put back together again. Unlike "Humpty Dumpty" who could not be put back together even with all the king's men—our heart has already been restored by the King. The "King of Glory," Jesus, has already done everything that needs to be done to establish our heart bringing us to maturity in Christ so we can live the "abundant" life He preached.

Recently, I was studying and I read a Scripture I am sure I had read prior, but this time the revelation of what God desires us to look like in our thoughts and our character became clear to me. "You, therefore, must be perfect [growing into complete maturity of godliness in mind and character, having reached the proper height of virtue and integrity], as your heavenly Father is perfect" (Matthew 5:48, Amplified).

An example of this is the Apostle Paul who reached the goal given to him by God. This is the picture of the believer who is full grown or of full age in both mind and character. This does not mean God's entire grace was given to Paul; what it means, however, is it was available and there was nothing deficient in his character morally. Paul did what God had for him to do in the manner God asked of him. This is why Paul could say "For I am already being poured out as a drink offering, and the time of my departure is at hand. I have fought the good fight, I have finished the race, I have kept the faith. Finally, there is laid up for me the crown of righteousness, which the Lord, the righteous Judge, will give to me on that Day, and not to me only but also to all who have loved His appearing" (2 Timothy 4:6–8).

However, we know Paul was not without challenges in his ministry and like King David, Paul was quick to repent and did not seem to hold a grudge toward those who wronged him. This is a sign of maturity—when we show no animosity, envy, dislike, malice, resentment or even hard feelings toward those saved as well as the unsaved. Our maturity is corresponding or appropriate to what God plans are for us, and should not be taken lightly because as we mature in Christ, the plan becomes even more apparent.

Four processes that can help bring the heart to this kind of maturity are: inner healing, meditating on the Word, declaring the Word, and doing the Word. These four areas will help us to accept what the Lord has already completed in us—a finished work!

Inner Healing

Just what is inner healing anyway? This question is usually given the response that inner healing is the believer allowing the working of the Holy Spirit to weed out all the wounds and pains from the past and bring forgiveness and healing in those areas. This is a good definition, but the simplest definition is "deliverance." Inner healing is deliverance. It is not only deliverance from those pains and wounds that are obvious, but those wounds that are concealed and secret to only us... so we think!

Inner healing is deliverance.

The fact of the matter is this whole book is about deliverance. It is about us allowing deliverance to come into our minds, will and emotions on a daily basis. I used to believe that deliverance was simply laying hands on someone and deliverance would come. This is the furthest thing from the truth. The truth of the matter is I can lay hands on you all day long, but if you choose not to receive or be delivered, then I have wasted a great deal of my time, which by the way is extremely valuable to me.

Years ago I was studying the Word of God and I asked the Lord why everyone He ministered to was delivered. He spoke to my heart and said "Because they wanted to be delivered." There were cities Jesus could not minister in, but those places that He did *all* were healed, delivered and totally set free. I believe this is the Kingdom of Heaven in operation on earth. Deliverance is not casting out demons especially in believers. Deliverance for the believer is daily allowing those things in the heart that are not like Christ to be put to death in our thoughts, conversations, and actions.

For whatever reason, we sometimes think only those who have additive behavior need deliverance. We need only look to First Corinthians to ascertain that this is not true. In the Epistles written by Paul we see him encouraging the believers to exemplify Christ not only in word but in their actions as well. When we truly experience inner healing our actions match what comes out of our mouths. I oversee our Children's Ministry at Way of Life and I tell parents their children not only hear what they say, but more importantly they watch what they do. Our behavior patterns are developed more by what we see demonstrated than what we are told that is not demonstrated.

As we previously talked about, adversities are going to come even for those who allow the Holy Spirit to bring deliverance to their heart, but we do not have to surrender to the circumstances. In fact, Hebrews 12:3 tells how to handle discouragement. "For consider Him who endured such hostility from sinners against Himself, lest you become weary and discouraged in your souls." When discouragement comes, think about what Christ has done for you, and will continue to do for you. This is what Matthew 5:48 means when it says we are to be mature in our mind and character with the word *perfect* in this Scripture meaning "mature."

Also, Hebrews 12:1 is saying to us—press on! "Therefore we also, since we are surrounded by so great a cloud of witnesses, let us lay aside every weight, and the sin which so easily ensnares us, and let us run with endurance the race that is set before us." These great clouds of witnesses are those who went before us spoken about in Hebrews chapter eleven; the Heroes of Faith. This Scripture tells us that their testimony surrounds us with encouragement letting us know unquestionably we can make it just as they did. What Abraham, Isaac, Jacob, Joseph, Moses, Rahab, Gideon, Barak, Samson, Jephthal, David and Samuel are all saying to us today is "If we did it you can also. We had no more skills than you—probably even less, but by faith we got it done."

They got it done even though they did not have the best— the promise we received. "And all these having obtained a good testimony through faith, did not receive the promise, God having provided something better for us, that they should not be made perfect apart from us" (Hebrews 11:39–40). Hallelujah!!! God provided something better for us, and His name is Jesus. So the next time you are discouraged, consider Him. Think on Him and His goodness towards you continuously.

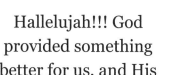

> Hallelujah!!! God provided something better for us, and His name is Jesus.

His goodness is His mercy, "Through the Lord's mercies we are not consumed, because His compassions fail not. They are new every morning; Great is [His] faithfulness" (Lamentations 3:23, Emphasis added).

This, thinking on the goodness of God, should be daily practice for us. If we want to maintain and keep the healing God has provided through His Son, Jesus, reminding ourselves of His goodness and praising Him has to be a way of life. A good way to remember is to make a habit of first waking up in the morning, finding a quiet place, putting in our ear plugs and listening to praise and worship music that ushers in the presence of God. This will set the tone for the day. No one or nothing else should control our day. The Lord provided both physical and inner healing on the Cross. In fact, the Lord did not make a distinction between the two; He simply provided salvation which means wholeness in every area of life.

Meditating on the Word

We talked a little about meditation in the previous chapters; however, it is important to investigate further what the Word of God says about meditation. The Scripture that first comes to mind is Joshua 1:8, "This Book of the Law shall not depart from your mouth, but you shall meditate in it day and night, that you may observe to do according to all that is written in it. For then you will make your way prosperous, and then you will have good success."

Here is Joshua successor to Moses being given instructions by God. In these instructions God tells Joshua that His Law will not depart from his mouth and he would meditate (murmur, mutter, sigh, moan, roar, speak, growl, whisper) the Word day and night. The Lord is telling Joshua that the Word will come out of him like the sound of a morning dove or the growling of a lion which has trapped its prey. Psalm 119:15 expresses meditation similarly yet differently: "I will meditate on Your precepts, and contemplate Your ways."

Here the word *meditation* means to ponder, to muse, to declare, to speak, to talk, to converse (aloud or even with oneself—utter with the mouth). And Isaiah 53:8 expresses meditating similar in that it means to consider, think upon something—going over a matter in one's mind, rehearsing it inwardly and outwardly.

My point is this: it is not enough to read and study the Word, we also must do as God instructed Joshua—murmur, speak, declare, ponder and rehearse the Word on a continual basis. I recently told someone, "Instead of trying to memorize numerous Scriptures, find one or two Scriptures and meditate on those until they consume your heart—until you know that you know you know!" An example of this continues to be demonstrated by Dr. Fred Price of Crenshaw Christian Center in Los Angeles. Here is a man who has not only declared, spoken, pondered, murmured and thought upon a Scripture rehearsing it over and over again, "For we walk by faith, not by sight," he in my opinion has *lived* this Scripture. If we can *truly* just get one Scripture in its fullness, there would be a transformation in our heart that no devil in hell could stop.

"Beloved," understand living a religious life does not benefit you in your heart or your soul. Pretending that we know the Word of God when in reality we do not only prolongs the agony that we are experiencing in our hearts. When we truly know the Word of God, it will rise to the top every time our soul has need of it. The Word will speak loud and clear from our hearts shutting down the negative emotions before they even have a chance to manifest.

Declaring the Word of God

Declaring the Word of God, simply put, is another form of meditation, and since words govern the earth it is advantageous for us to declare the Word of God in and over our lives. Why would I say that words govern the earth? Because when we read

Genesis 1:2b we see that the "Spirit of God was hovering over the face of the waters." However, it was not until God spoke that it was. What was? "Then God said, 'Let there be light'; and there was light" (Genesis 1:3).

When we look at the words *be* and *was* they are the same word in the Hebrew, but notice the word *was* is past tense letting us know that the light already was! We also know that light already existed because God Himself is light, but the manifestation of this light upon the earth did not occur until God *spoke*. Additional meanings of these two words are to breathe, to exist, and to be. Hallelujah! As soon as God opened His mouth, it manifested.

Declaring the Word of God in our lives is just that powerful. Sometime in the 70's I read a book entitled *Hung by the Tongue* and I have since read it several more times. James 3:10 tells us, "Out of the same mouth proceed blessing and cursing. My brethren these things ought not to be so." James tells us only blessings should come forth out of our mouth. This includes declaring blessings over our own life.

Speaking the Word over ourselves and others is so important that we instruct people to pray the Word of God when they pray for others. We tell them to pray as little as possible of their own thoughts, ideas, and opinions because only the Word of God is true—nothing else matters. Our thoughts, our ideas, and our opinions will return void, but God's Word will not return unto Him void, it shall accomplish what He please, and it shall prosper in the thing for which He sent it (Isaiah 55:11).

Notice that Isaiah 55:11 clearly states that God's Word will not return unto Him void. If you desire to see your broken heart healed and not experience emotional ups and downs, declare the

Word of God over yourself. Find the area in the Word of God that pertains to your situation and declare what God's Word says about you in the midst of the pain. I continue to learn that God's Word exceeds anything I could possibly imagine.

Doing the Word of God

This is where the "rubber meets the road." We are to do what the Word of God tells us regardless of the cost, and it cost us to do the Word as well as to not do the Word. The difference being the price we pay.

Let us look at a group of people in the Word that were not doers of the Word and what it cost them for being disobedient, for to not do the Word is disobedience on our part and either way there is a price to pay.

And the Lord said: I have surely seen the oppression of My people who are in Egypt, and have heard their cry because of their taskmasters, for I know their sorrows. So I have come down to deliver them out of the hand of the Egyptians, and to bring them up from that land to a good and large land, to a land flowing with milk and honey, to the place of the Canaanites and the Hittites and the Amorites and Perizzites and the Hivites and the Jebusites (Exodus 3:7–8).

Now picture this...

The God that has been talked about from generation to

generation is about to deliver (snatch you out of, draw you out of, save you, set you free, withdraw you, cause you to escape) from the hands of the unrighteous and bring you up from (cause you to ascend, mount up, go up, grow up, be exalted, taken away, removed) the land of bondage to a large (roomy in every direction, broad, wide, place of liberty) place that flows with milk (richness, best, fat, choice part, finest) and honey (sweet place, dear place, flowery place).

Would your question be, *What do I have to do?* Glad you ask that question. Exodus 19:5–8 gives us the answer:

> *Now therefore, if you will indeed obey My voice and keep My covenant, then you shall be a special treasure to Me above all people; for all the earth is Mine. And you shall be to Me a kingdom of priests and a holy nation. These are the words which you shall speak to the children of Israel. So Moses came and called for the elders of the people, and laid before them all these words which the Lord commanded him. Then all the people answered together and said, "All that the Lord has spoken we will do." So Moses brought back the words of the people to the Lord.*

When you read further in Exodus 24:7–8, you can see that the Lord made a covenant with Israel and they affirmed the covenant. Moses went to meet with God on Mt. Sinai at least seven times, but he did not stay forty days and forty nights. It was only on the fifth trip to the Mt. Sinai during which Moses spent forty days and forty nights, and it was during the fifth trip that the Ten Commandments were given by God to Moses.

Moses was gone forty days and forty nights and while he was on Mt. Sinai he wrote all that God gave him. However, it was not just the Ten Commandments that were given; the instructions for the offering in the sanctuary; instructions for the Ark of the Testimony and all its items; instructions on the Tabernacle, instructions on the garment for the Priesthood and consecration of the Priest; the anointing oil, bronze laver; the incense, the artisan for building the Tabernacle and the Sabbath Law.

Here is Moses writing every Word God had given him (Exodus 24:4a) and the people decide to make their own "gods" and then have a party:

> *Now when the people saw that Moses delayed coming down from the mountain, the people gathered together to Aaron, and said to him, "Come, make us gods that shall go before us, for as for this Moses, the man who brought us up out of the land of Egypt, we do not know what has become of him." Then they rose early on the next day, offered burnt offerings, and brought peace offerings; and the people sat down to eat and drink, and rose up to play* (Exodus 32:1,6).

No wonder Moses was upset. I would be upset also after spending forty days and nights writing every word God gave to return to the people and find them worshipping idols and partying. Moses was so upset he broke the tablets of stone God made on Mt. Sinai. The Israelites had seen God not only deliver them out of Egypt, but provide for them time and time again as well. Yet, because of their hearts they could not keep God's Covenant. You can read in Exodus 34 where God had Moses make new tablets of stone, and He rewrites what was on the first tablets.

The whole point in looking at the disobedience of the Israelites is for us to understand what their disobedience cost them. God promised them the best of the best even before they left Egypt. He not only promised them the best, He provided everything they needed while in their wilderness journey which is what He has done for us—given us His best and provided all that we need. God sent His best, Jesus, to die for us (John 3:16), but we have to make the decision to come out of Egypt in order to receive His best. We must not do what the Israelites did—be brought out of Egypt only to die in the wilderness.

The journey from Egypt to the Promised Land which should have taken no more than eleven days took Israel forty years, and all those twenty years and older except Caleb and Joshua never saw the Promised Land (Numbers 14:29–30). Those that rebelled lost everything. What is important for us to understand is that it does not take a long time to get what God has promised. What it takes is obedience to receive what He has promised. This type of obedience will not come forth in an immature heart. What God desires for us is a mature heart!

When we receive inner healing, meditate on the Word, declare the Word, and do the Word, our hearts mature and function in the manner God intended. We must understand that maturity of heart is not how many Scriptures we can quote or even how anointed we are in flowing in the Gifts of the Spirit. True maturity is godliness in our thoughts and our patterns of behavior. Notice how Matthew 5:43–48 tells us that, alone, neither our thoughts nor behavioral patterns demonstrate maturity—it is both together that brings maturity of the heart. What this tells us is there is a hearing of the Word (thoughts) and a doing of the Word (pattern of behavior).

Thousands of thoughts enter our minds daily; however, we decide what to absorb or reject. The quicker we decide the less chance negative thoughts have of controlling our emotions. If we let negative thoughts control our emotions than some form of action is sure to follow. For example, you are taking an exam, and a thought pops into your head, *cheat!* You either dismiss the thought immediately or you entertain the thought momentarily. Then the moment turns into minutes with an ongoing focus to cheat. If we never shut the negative thought down, it will keep generating steam until it manifests. At some point we must say no to the negative thoughts.

> What is important for us to understand is that it does not take a long time to get what God has promised. What it takes is obedience to receive what He has promised.

This might be an over simplified example, but it is exactly what happens when we are processing thoughts. This is why it is important to have the Word of God in our hearts so that as these negative thoughts come—the heart which is full of the Word comes to our aid and now our spirits tell the rest of our members how they are going to respond. Now it is the Word which generates stream until it manifest.

This is why Jesus came, so we would no longer be ruled or controlled by our flesh causing us to live a sinful life. We now have full access to grace and truth in our hearts. Grace—this wonderful ability of God on the inside of us helping us to do what we are unable to do ourselves, and the truth which is behind God's ability on the inside of us!!!

Why is it important for us to mature spiritually? We have covered a few, but the most important in my opinion is the plan of God for our lives. God has always and will continue to look for obedience from His people. Have you ever heard it said that God does not need you? Yes He does! He not only needs us, He desires to use us for His glory and for our good. When we study the Word, we find God seeking those who will obey Him. The plan of God for His kingdom on earth has not changed; therefore, He still needs and desires obedient men, women, boys and girls to establish His kingdom here on earth. "Your kingdom come, your will be done on earth as it is in heaven" (Matthew 6:10). Let us look at some benefits to maturing spiritually that assist the plan of God for His will to be done on earth.

Wisdom

When we are spiritually mature we easily partake of God's wisdom:

However, we speak wisdom among those who are mature, yet not the wisdom of this age, nor of the rulers of this age, who are coming to nothing. But we speak the wisdom of God in a mystery, the hidden wisdom which God ordained before the ages for our glory, which none of the rulers of this age knew; for had they known, they would not have crucified the Lord of glory. But as it is written: "Eye has not seen, nor ear heard, nor have entered into the heart of man the things which God has prepared for those who love Him" (1 Corinthians 2:6–9).

When we are spiritually mature we will hear the wisdom of God come forth when others are speaking. This Scripture is clearly saying that this wisdom is not from man or those in high places, but this wisdom is from God and only those that are mature will understand its contents for it is spoken in secret. It is for those who are willing to pay the price through obedience bringing growth and understanding to their soul changing their heart to reflect Christ with all His attributes. It is not for those who want a quick word from someone, or those who choose not to spend time in the Word and prayer.

Also notice in verse seven, this wisdom was predetermined for our glory long before we came on the scene. This is awesome! This means that God knew that we would be here for such a time as this. We get to walk in obedience and participate in God's plan for our lives. Verse nine tells us that we cannot even lay hold of all the plans He has anticipated for us. Think about it. If you have children or plan to have children, this is you thinking years in advance of what you want to see your children become or what you want their lives to reflect. So you

> We get to walk in obedience and participate in God's plan for our lives.

begin to make plans in advance—establishing a secure foundation for your children long before they arrive. Verse two tells us that

God destined this for our glory. What a privilege to serve a God who has already planned my life leaving me the responsibility only to walk in obedience of what He directs me to do.

Pressing Forward

Not that I have already attained, or am already perfected; but I press on, that I may lay hold of that for which Christ Jesus has also laid hold of me. Brethren, I do not count myself to have apprehended; but one thing I do, forgetting those things which are behind and reaching forward to those things which are ahead, I press toward the goal for the prize of the upward call of God in Christ Jesus. Therefore let us, as many as are mature, have this mind; and if in anything you think otherwise, God will reveal even this to you (Philippians 3:12–15).

One of the things that demonstrates an *eclipsed heart* is the inability to move forward. When we are not able to let go of past hurts and pains, we consciously or subconsciously make the decision to stop our growth. Paul is telling the Philippian Church that perfection or maturity comes as we continue to move forward. It is not healthy to spiritually, physically, mentally or emotionally rehearse past disappointments. In chapter four we talked about the mind being similar to a record that played on a phonograph or record player which is what we called it years ago. Everything that we have mentally, physically and emotionally retained and experienced in our life has made grooves in our mind (the record), but these grooves can be reversed.

Not rehearsing the past in thought, conversation and actions along with allowing the Word of God to make new grooves is how we are able to reverse the negative thoughts. Paul says forget those things that are behind us not letting them control who we are or where we are going. Always remember we are never standing still we are either moving forward or going backward. Yes, we find ourselves having a battle with our emotions when we are serious about moving forward, but the alternative to pressing is not an option if we want to say what Paul said, "I have finished the race" (2 Timothy 4:7).

Practicing the Truth

Knowing the Word and speaking the Word can never substitute for doing the Word. In the book of James, the mature believer also does what the Word says. It is not good enough to be able to quote the Word, we must also apply the Word. The Apostle James uses favoritism to help bring practicing the truth out:

My brethren, do not hold the faith of our Lord Jesus Christ, the Lord of glory, with partiality. For if there should come into your assembly a man with gold rings, in fine apparel, and there should also come in a poor man in filthy clothes, and you pay attention to the one wearing the fine clothes and say to him, "You sit here in a good place," and say to the poor man, "You stand there," or, "Sit here at my footstool," have you not shown partiality among yourselves, and become judges with evil thoughts? (James 2:1–4)

The context of this passage deals with how we should treat one another. Here, James is focusing on the intent of our hearts. This is one of the differences between the Old and the New Covenant—meaning the intention behind what we do. Have you ever helped someone and then complained? Our motives must be right whether we are asked or we volunteer to assist someone. In fact if we do it and complain, we undermine the heart's genuine purpose for helping.

Our heart is protected when we do things properly because the New Covenant which was a better covenant brought both grace and truth. This means with God's ability in us helping us to do what we are unable to do ourselves things get done in His strength with the appropriate motive and right attitude. If we treat the poor man differently simply because he is poor, we are mistreating him and the problem rests in our hearts. Even when it looks good outwardly, it is still a problem; for what God is concerned about is our inward appearance not our outward appearance. Living the truth is not a challenge, it is a decision!

It is a decision to be truthful no matter what the situation. King David asked the Lord and the Lord responded:

Lord, who shall dwell [temporarily] in Your tabernacle? Who shall dwell [permanently] on Your holy hill? He who walks and lives uprightly and blamelessly, who works rightness and justice and speaks and thinks the truth in his heart, He who does not slander with his tongue, nor does evil to his friend, nor takes up a reproach against his neighbor (Psalm 15:1–3, Amplified).

Living truthfully is not something we get to wear when it is convenient. It is something that we do honoring our God and giving Him glory. Not honoring self but honoring the Lord by showing the world we live life with a standard far above worldly concepts of acceptance. A standard set by our heavenly Father. A standard that cannot be duplicated by the world no matter how hard the world tries; we will remain out of reach in comparison to the world in our thoughts, speech, and actions. We are to live life in such a manner that the world comes to the Church for correction and guidance. How would you like for those on your job to seek you out for the wisdom of God in both personal and work issues. Imagine prophesying giving a Word of Knowledge or Word of Wisdom in a life and death situation, with the person seeking you out for a solution to their problem.

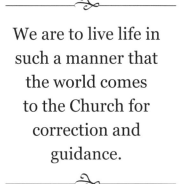

We are to live life in such a manner that the world comes to the Church for correction and guidance.

Only the mature heart is open and ready for opportunities like this which will bring glory to God. Remember all that we do is for our good and His glory. We must allow the Holy Spirit of truth to show us those moments when we are not truthful or we embellish facts trying to impress those around us in an attempt to demonstrate our knowledge or that we are competent. Jesus said in John 3:32, "And you shall know the truth, and the truth shall make you free." Free from what? Free from the bondage of sin. "Most assuredly, I say to you, whoever commits sin is a slave of sin. And a slave does not abide in the house forever, but a son abides forever. Therefore if the Son makes you free, you shall be free indeed" (John 8:34–36).

Casts out Fear

"There is no fear in love; but perfect love casts out fear, because fear involves torment. But he who fears has not been made perfect in love" (1 John 4:18). I find this Scripture to be simply wonderful. Why? Because it tells me I am in control of whether or not fear operates in my heart. When we have perfect love or mature love in our heart fear cannot stay—it cannot torment us. On the flip side, if we do have fear it will bring frustration, agony, distress, anguish, affliction, misery, pain and suffering to our hearts leaving us paralyzed and incapacitated. This Scripture is telling us to allow love to prefect our hearts or mature our hearts so we can be free from all fear.

Notice that it did not say have someone cast the spirit of fear out of us—it directs us to deal with our hearts allowing the Holy Spirit to search for anything that is not like God. Loving those who have wronged us may not be easy, but it is accomplishable. God did it and He continues to do it every day—loving us in spite of our wrongs and disobedience towards Him. He is not asking us to do something He has not already done. Thank God we are not powerless in these matters. "For God has not given us a spirit of fear, but of power and of love and of a sound mind" (1 Timothy 1:7). This is the power of the Holy Spirit for Acts 1:8 tells us, "But you shall receive power when the Holy Spirit has come upon you; and you shall be witnesses to Me in Jerusalem, and in all Judea and Samaria, and to the end of the earth." This power is not only for witnessing it is power for service, but service first must start in a heart of love because if it does not our motives for doing will not be consistent with the truth Jesus brought us in the New Covenant.

I see truth and love as being synonymous. We cannot have one without the other because Christ is both—truth and love. I am not speaking of just telling the truth, although telling the truth is important. I am speaking about the condition of the heart—a heart that is both truthful and loving. A simple way to test our spiritual maturity is to ask ourselves, *Am I slow to speak? Do I love easily? Do I give easily and repent quickly?* We can list many other variables to test our spiritual maturity, but when we tally it up most of what is said would probably

> I see truth and love as being synonymous.

fall under one of these four categories. Take a moment and honestly access yourself. Even as I am writing, I know there are areas in my spiritual walk that need my attention.

We must let the love of God which is in our heart cause us to respond truthfully. In so doing we will not only demonstrate maturity to those around us we also will reveal and teach the correct way to live—God's way of life. "He will teach us His ways, and we shall walk in His paths" (Isaiah 2:3).

Heart Meditation Devotional
Scriptural Emphasis Added[1]

In Joshua 1:8 we are told, "This Book of the Law shall not depart from your mouth, but you shall meditate in it day and night, that you may observe to do according to all that is written in it. For then you will make your way prosperous, and then you will have good success." What Joshua was told then is the same for us today. The journey, the walk, the road, our way of life will be prosperous (push forward, come mightily, be profitable) as we meditate on God's Word day and night bringing us good success (to be successful, acting in a prosperous manner). Find a quiet place to come along side of me as we meditate on the Word of God and explore the deepest areas of our hearts in our personal devotional time. You will experience and be able to declare that God's Words "...*are* life to those who find them, and health to all their flesh" (Proverbs 4:22).

The Heartfelt Devotional

"Therefore know this day, and consider it in your heart, that the Lord Himself is God in heaven above and on the earth beneath there is no other" (Deuteronomy 4:39).

"Therefore you shall lay up these words of mine in your heart and in your soul, and bind them as a sign on your hand, [showing direction,] and they shall be as frontlets or restrained, fastened between your eyes, [your countenance]" (Deuteronomy 11:18).

"This day the Lord your God commands you to observe these statues and judgments; therefore you shall be careful to observe them with all your heart and with all your soul" (Deuteronomy 26:16).

"And the Lord your God will circumcise your heart and the heart of your descendants, to love the Lord your God with all your heart and with all your soul, that you may live" (Deuteronomy 30:6).

"My heart rejoices in the Lord" (1 Samuel 2:1).

"Only fear, [*reverence*] the Lord, and serve Him in truth with all your heart; for consider what great things He has done for you" (1 Samuel 12:24).

"For the Lord does not see as man sees, for man looks at the outward appearance, but the Lord looks at the heart" (1 Samuel 16:7b).

"Go do all that is in your heart, for the Lord is with you" (2 Samuel 7:3b).

"...give to your servant an understanding [*and a discerning*] heart" (1 Kings 3:9a).

"Lord God of Israel, there is no God in heaven above or on earth below like You, who keep Your covenant and mercy with Your servants who walk before You with all their hearts" (1 Kings 8:23).

"Let your heart therefore be loyal to the Lord our God, to walk in His statutes, [*decrees, His set time,*] and keep His commandments, as at this day, [*this season, this process of time*]" (1 Kings 8:61).

"Remember now, O Lord, I pray, how I have walked before You in truth and with a loyal heart, and have done what was good in Your sight, [*Your countenance*]" (2 Kings 20:3).

"Glory in His holy name; let the hearts of those rejoice who seek the Lord" (1 Chronicles 16:10).

"Now set your heart and your soul to seek the Lord your God" (1 Chronicles 22:19a).

"Then the people rejoiced, for they had offered willingly, because with a loyal heart they had offered willingly to the Lord" (1 Chronicles 29:9).

"I know also, my God, that You test the heart and have pleasure in uprightness, [*equity.*] As for me, in the uprightness, [*equity of my heart*] I have willingly offered all these things; and now with joy I have seen Your people, who are present here to offer willingly to You" (1 Chronicles 29:17).

"O Lord God of Abraham, Isaac, and Israel, our fathers, keep this forever in the intent of the thoughts of the heart of Your people, and fix their heart toward You" (1 Chronicles 29:18).

"[*I*] prepared [*my*] heart to seek the Law of the Lord, and do it, and to teach His statutes and ordinances in Israel" (Ezra 7:10).[2]

"What is man, that You should exalt him, that You should set Your heart on him?" (Job 7:17)

"God is wise in heart and mighty in strength, Who has hardened himself against Him and prospered?" (Job 9:4)

"Receive, please, instruction from His mouth, and lay up His words [*advice and answers*] in your heart" (Job 22:22).

"My righteousness I hold fast, and will not let it go; My heart shall not reproach [*rebuke, scold*] *me* as long as I live" (Job 27:6).

"My words come from my upright heart; My lips utter pure knowledge" (Job 33:3).

"As for the Almighty, we cannot find Him; He is excellent in power, in judgment and abundant justice; He does not oppress. Therefore men fear [*reverence*]

Him; He shows no partiality to any who are wise of heart" (Job 37:23–24).

"My defense is of God, who saves [*delivers, gave victory to*] the upright [*the pleasing, the agreeing*] in heart" (Psalm 7:10).

"I will praise You [*give thanks to you, sing to you*], O Lord, with my whole heart; I will tell of all Your marvelous [*Your extraordinary, Your wonderful, miraculous*] works" (Psalm 9:1).

"I have trusted in Your mercy; My heart shall rejoice in Your salvation" (Psalm 13:5).

"Let the words of my mouth and the meditation of my heart be acceptable [*be delightful, find favor*] in Your sight [*in Your presence*], O Lord, my strength and my Redeemer [*my Avenger, my Deliverer*]" (Psalm 19:14).

"May He grant [*me, give me, put me, make me*] according to my heart's desire, and fulfill [*confirm, accomplish*] all [*my*] purpose" (Psalm 20:4).[3]

"Examine [*test*] me, O Lord, and prove me; try [*refine, purify*] my mind and my heart" (Psalm 26:2).

"Though an army may encamp against me, my heart shall not [*shall never*] fear [*shall never be afraid*]; Though war may rise against me, in this I will be confident" (Psalm 27:3).

"Wait [*trust, look patiently*] on the Lord [*expect the Lord*]; be of good [*strong*] courage, and He shall strengthen your heart; wait [*trust*], I say, on the Lord!" (Psalm 27:14)

"The Lord is my strength and my shield; my heart trusted [*is sure, has confidence*] in Him, and I am helped; Therefore my heart greatly rejoices, and with my song I will praise Him" (Psalm 28:7).

"Be of good courage [*be strong, be constant, be established*], and He shall strengthen your heart, all you who hope in the Lord" (Psalm 31:24).

"The counsel [*the advice*] of the Lord stands forever, the plans [*the intentions, and the thoughts*] of His heart to all generations" (Psalm 33:11).

"He fashions [*squeezes into shape, molds into a form*] their hearts individually; He considers [*understands, directs, discerns, and instructs*] all their works" (Psalm 33:15).

"For our heart shall rejoice in Him, because we have trusted [*are sure of, have confidence*] in His holy name" (Psalm 33:21).

"The Lord is near to those who have a broken heart [*a*

hurt heart, a crushed heart], and saves [*delivers, gives victory to*] such as have a contrite [*destructive*] spirit" (Psalm 34:18).

"Oh, continue Your loving kindness [*your favor, your good deeds, your mercy*] to those who know You, and Your righteousness [*Your justice*] to the upright in heart" (Psalm 36:10).

"Delight yourself also in the Lord, and He shall give you [*with the greatest latitude of application*] the desires of your heart" (Psalm 37:4).

"The law [*percepts, statutes*] of [*my*] God are in my heart; none of [*my*] steps shall slide [*waver or slip*]" (Psalm 37:31).[4]

"I delight [*I bend, I desire and I have pleasure*] to do Your will, O my God, and Your law [*Your precepts, Your statutes*] is within my heart" (Psalm 40:8).

"For He knows [*acknowledges, advises, and answers*] the secrets of the heart" (Psalm 44:21b).

"My mouth shall speak [*shall command, shall declare, shall promise, shall rehearse*] wisdom, and the meditation of my heart shall give understanding [*skillfulness, reason, discretion, wisdom*]" (Psalm 49:3).

"Create in me a clean [*pure, fair*] heart, O God, and renew a steadfast [*established, fixed, prepared*] spirit within me [*my inward parts, my thoughts*]" (Psalm 51:10).

"My heart is steadfast [*established and sure*], O God, my heart is steadfast [*established and sure*]; I will sing and give praise" (Psalm 57:7).

"Trust in [*be sure of and have confidence in*] the Lord at all times, you people; pour out your heart before Him; God is a refuge for us" (Psalm 62:8).

"The righteous [*the just*] shall be glad in the Lord, and trust [*confide, and have hope*] in Him. And all the upright [*just*] in heart shall glory [*boast, rave and celebrate*]" (Psalm 64:10).

"God is the strength of my heart and my portion [*my inheritance, my allotment*] forever [*for eternity*]" (Psalm 73:26b).

"I call to remembrance my song in the night [*in my adversity*]; I meditate within my heart, and my spirit makes diligent search" (Psalm 77:6).

"My soul longs, yes, even faints [*ceases*] for the courts of the Lord; my heart and my flesh cry out for the living God" (Psalm 84:2).

"Blessed [*and happy*] is the man whose strength is in You,

whose heart is set on pilgrimage [*the course and path*]"
(Psalm 84:5).

"Teach me Your way, O Lord; I will walk [*the course of life*] in Your truth; unite my heart to fear Your name. I will praise You, O Lord my God, with all my heart, and I will glorify Your name forevermore" (Psalm 86:11–12).

"But judgment will return to righteousness [*to equity, to prosperity*] and all the upright, [*just*] in heart will follow it" (Psalm 94:15).

"Light [*clarity, brightness, and the morning*] is sown for the righteous [*the just*] and gladness for the upright [*just, straight*] in heart" (Psalm97:11).

"I will walk [*grow, lead, march, behave*] within my house with a perfect heart" (Psalm 101:2b).

"Glory in His Holy name; let the hearts of those rejoice who seek the Lord" (Psalm 105:3).

"With my whole heart I have sought You; oh, let me not wander [*go astray, deceive, or sin through ignorance*] from Your commandments" (Psalm 119:10).

 "Your word I have hidden in my heart, that I might not sin against You" (Psalm 119:11).

"I will praise [*the Lord*] with my whole heart" (Psalm 138:1a).[5]

"He heals [*thoroughly makes whole*] the brokenhearted and binds [*wraps thoroughly and stops*] up their wounds [*their pain and their sorrow*]" (Psalm 147:3).

"When wisdom [*the ability to live life skillfully*] enters [*my*] heart, and knowledge is pleasant to [*my*] soul [*mind, will, emotions*], discretion [*a plan, witty invention, a good thought*] will preserve [*me*]; understanding [*reason, skillfulness*] will keep [*me*]" (Proverbs 2:10–11).[6]

"My son, do not forget my law, but let your heart keep my commands; for length of days and long life and peace [*well, happy, healthy, and prosperity*] they will add to you" (Proverbs 3:1–2).

"Trust *be confident, be sure and be bold* in the Lord with all your heart and lean not on your own understanding *or knowledge*; in all your ways acknowledge, *know Him,* and He shall direct, *make right, make straight, make pleasant and prosperous* your paths (Proverbs 3:5-6).

"Keep [*guard, maintain and obey*] your heart with all diligence, for out of it spring the issues of life" (Proverbs 4:23).

"A sound [*a cured, a healed, a delivered, a whole*] heart is life to [*my*] body" (Proverbs 14:30a).[7]

"Wisdom [*the ability to live life skillfully*] rests in the heart of him who has understanding [*cunningness, diligence, directness, eloquence and discernment*]" (Proverbs 14:33a).

"The heart of him who has understanding [*cunningness, diligence, eloquence and discernment*] seeks knowledge" (Proverbs 15:14a).

"He who is of a merry [*a good, a beautiful, a cheerful, an at ease, and a bountiful*] heart has a continual [*a perpetual*] feast" (Proverbs 15:15b).

"The heart of the righteous [*the just*] studies [*ponders imagines, meditates, mourns, mutters, roars and speaks*] how to answer" (Proverbs 15:28a).

"The light [*the cheerfulness, the brightness of the eyes*] rejoices the heart, and a good [*a joyful, a merry, a pleasant, and a bountiful*] report makes the bones [*the body, life*] healthy [*and anointed*]" (Proverbs 15:30).

"The preparations [*mental dispositions*] of the heart belong to man, but the answer of the tongue is from the Lord" (Proverbs 16:1).

A man's heart plans [*weaves, plots, fabricates, contrives, computes, regards, values, and interpenetrate*s] his way [*his course of life or mode of action*] but the Lord directs his steps (Proverbs 16:9).

The wise [*the skillful*] in heart will be called prudent [*direct, cunning, diligent, eloquent and discerning*], and sweetness of the lips [*speech, talk*] increases learning [*instruction, doctrine*] (Proverbs 16:21).

The heart of the wise [*skillful at heart*] teaches [*and instructs*] his mouth [*to behave*], and adds learning to his lips [*speech, talk*] (Proverbs 16:23).

A merry [*a glad, a joyful*] heart does good, like a medicine [*a cure*], but a broken spirit dries the bones [*the body*] (Proverbs 17:22).

He who loves purity of heart and has grace [*kindness and favor*] on his lips [*his speech, his language*], the king will be his friend [*his companion and close associate*] (Proverbs 22:11).

Apply your heart to instruction [*correction, doctrine*], and your ears [*your hearing*] to words [*answers*] of knowledge (Proverbs 23:12).

Do not let your heart envy [*be jealous of*] sinners [*offenders*], but be zealous for the fear [*reverence*] of the

Lord all the day (Proverbs 23:17).

Hear [*be obedient, listen, perceive*] my son, and be wise; and guide [*prosper, lead*] your heart in the way (Proverbs 23:19).

My son, give [*apply, appoint, assign*] me your heart, and let your eyes [*your countenance*] observe [*protect, maintain*] my ways (Proverbs 23:26).

Ointment and perfume delight the heart, and the sweetness of a man's friend [*companion, close associate*] gives delight by hearty counsel (Proverbs 27:9).

The heart of her husband safely trusts [*is secure, is sure of*] her; so he will have no lack of gain (Proverbs 31:11).

For [*I*] will not dwell unduly on the days of [*my*] life, because God keeps [*me*] busy with the joy of [*my*] heart (Ecclesiastes 5:20).[8]

I applied my heart to know [*to advise, to answer, to comprehend, to consider*] to search and seek out wisdom [*the ability to live life skillfully*] and the reason of things (Ecclesiastes 7:25a).

He who keeps [*guards, protects, attends*] his command will experience [*will know, will advise, will comprehend*] nothing harmful; and a wise [*skillful and intelligent*] man's heart discerns [*answers, advises and comprehends*] both time and judgment (Ecclesiastes 8:5).

For I considered [*applied, ascribed*] all this in my heart, so that I could declare it all: that the righteous [*just, lawful*] and the wise and their works are in the hand of God (Ecclesiastes 9:1).

Walk [*continually*] in the ways [*manner*] of your heart, and in the sight [*appearance*] of your eyes [*your countenance*] (Ecclesiastes 11:9b).

Therefore remove [*turn off, call back and decline*] sorrow [*anger, grief, indignation, provocation, spite, and wrath*] from your heart (Ecclesiastes 11:10a).

You shall have a song as in the night [*in adversity*] when a holy festival is kept, and gladness of heart as when one goes with a flute, to come into the mountain of the Lord (Isaiah 30:29).

Remember [*recognize, recount, record*] now, O Lord, I pray, how I have walked, [*behaved, exercised*] before You in truth and with a loyal heart, and have done what is good in Your sight, [*Your face*] (Isaiah 38:3).

Then you shall see [*consider, discern, experience*] and become radiant, and your heart shall swell with joy; because the abundance of the sea shall be turned to you, the wealth, [*army, valor, strength, goods, riches, might and substance of the Gentiles*] shall come to you (Isaiah 60:5).

Behold, My servants shall sing for joy of heart (Isaiah 65:14a).

I will give [*apply, appoint, assign, bestow, consider, commit*] to you shepherds according to My heart, who will feed you with knowledge and understanding [*expertise and prosperity*] (Jeremiah 3:15).

But You, O Lord, know [*recognize and acknowledge*] me, and You have tested, [*examined, proved*] my heart toward You (Jeremiah 12:3a).

Your words [*advice, and answers*] were found, and I ate them, and Your word [*your advice, your answer*] was to me the joy and rejoicing of my heart; for I am called by Your name, O Lord of hosts (Jeremiah 15:16).

The heart is deceitful [*polluted*] above all things, and desperately wicked; who can know it? I, the Lord search the heart, I test the mind, even to give [*apply, appoint, assign*] every man according to his ways [*his course of life, his mode*] of action according to the fruit of his doings (Jeremiah 17:9-10).

His word was in my heart like a burning fire shut up in

my bones [*my body*]; I was weary of holding it back, and I could not (Jeremiah 20:9b).

I will give [*apply, appoint, assign, bestow, consider and commit*] them a heart to know Me, that I am the Lord; and they shall be My people, and I will be their God, for they shall return to Me, with their whole heart (Jeremiah 24:7).

You will seek Me and find Me, when you search for Me with all your heart (Jeremiah 29:13).

I will give [*apply, appoint, assign, bestow on them*] one heart and one way, that they may fear Me forever, for the good of them and their children after them (Jeremiah 32:39).

I will make an everlasting [*eternal and continual*] covenant with them, that I will not turn away from doing them good; but I will put My fear in their hearts so that they will not depart from Me (Jeremiah 32:40).

I will rejoice over them to do them good, and I will assuredly [*firmly*] plant them in this land, with all My heart, and with all My soul (Jeremiah 32:41).

Arise, cry out in the night [*in adversity*] at the beginning [*at the forefront, at the height*] of the watches [*surveillance, vigil*]; pour out your heart like water before the face, [*the countenance*] of the Lord (Lamentations 2:19a).

Let us lift [*arise, advance, bring forth*] our hearts and hands to God in heaven (Lamentations 3:41).

Son of man, receive into your heart all My words [*my advice, my answers*] that I speak [*command, declare and pronounce*] to you, and hear with your ears (Ezekiel 3:10).

I will give [*apply, appoint, assign, bestow, consider, commit*] to them one heart, and I will put a new spirit within them and take the stony heart out of their flesh, [*their nakedness*] and give them a heart of flesh [*of nakedness*] (Ezekiel 11:19).

Cast away [*throw out, hurl, pluck out*] from you all the transgressions [*all rebellion*] which you have committed, and get yourselves a new heart and a new spirit (Ezekiel 18:31a).

I will give [*apply, appoint, assign, bestow, commit*] to you a new heart and put a new spirit within you; I will take the heart of stone out of your flesh and give you a heart of flesh (Ezekiel 36:26).

Do not fear [*be afraid, dread or be frightened*] Daniel, for from the first day that you set your heart to understand [*consider, direct, discern, feel, and inform*] and to humble yourself before your God, your words were heard; and I have come because of your words (Daniel 10:12).

Turn to Me with all your heart, with fasting, with weeping, and with mourning (Joel 2:12).

So rend [*cut out, tear*] your heart and not your garments [*clothing or robes*]; return to the Lord your God, for He is gracious and merciful (Joel 2:13a).

Sing, O daughter of Zion! Shout, O Israel! Be glad and rejoice with all your heart, O daughter of Jerusalem! (Zephaniah 3:14).

Blessed [*fortunate, well off, happy*] are the pure [*clean, and clear*] in heart, for they shall see God (Matthew 5:8).

For where your treasure [*wealth*] is, there your heart will be also (Matthew 6:21).

Take [*bear up, carry*] My yoke upon you and learn from Me, for I am gentle and lowly [*humble*] in heart, and you will find rest [*intermission*] for your souls (Matthew 11:29).

For out of the abundance [*that which has left over—superabundance*] of the heart the mouth speaks [*talks, tells, preaches*] (Matthew 12:34b).

A good [*well*] man out of the good [*wellness, treasure*] of his heart brings forth good things (Matthew 12:35a).

You shall love the Lord your God with all your heart [*whole heart*] with all your soul [*whole soul*], and with all your mind [*deep thought, imagination and understanding*] (Matthew 22:37).

For assuredly, I say to you, whoever says to this mountain [*as lifting it above the plain*], "Be removed and cast [*violently thrown into the sea*]" and does not doubt [*waver or stagger*] in his heart, but believes [*has faith in and commits*] to those things he says will be done, he will have whatever he says (Mark 11:23).

And you shall love the Lord your God with all your heart [*whole heart*] with all your soul [*with your entire mind*], and with all your strength (Mark 12:30).

And to love Him with all the heart, with all the understanding, with all the soul, and with all the strength [*power, might and ability*] and to love one's neighbor as oneself, is more than all the whole burnt offerings and sacrifices (Mark 12:33).

A good [*a well*] man out of the good treasure of his heart brings forth good [*wellness*] (Luke 6:45a).

Let not your heart be troubled; you believe in [*has faith in, commits to*] God, believe [*have faith in, commit*] also in Me (John 14:1).

Peace [*quietness, rest and prosperity*] I leave with you, My peace I give to you; not as the world gives do I give to you. Let not your heart be troubled, neither let it be afraid (John 14:27).

Therefore my heart rejoiced, and my tongue was glad; moreover my flesh also will rest in hope (Acts 2:26).

Now the multitude of those who believed were of one heart and one soul (Acts 4:32a).

The word is near you, in your mouth and in your heart (that is the word of faith which we preach [*have faith in, commit to*]): that if you confess [*acknowledge*] with your mouth the Lord Jesus and believe in your heart that God has raised Him from the dead, you will be saved [*made whole, healed, preserved*]. For with the heart one believes [*has faith in, commit to*] unto righteousness, and with the mouth confession [*covenant, promise*] is made unto salvation [*health, safety and deliverance*] (Romans 10:8–10).

Eye has not seen [*known, considered or perceived*] nor ear heard [*understood*] nor have entered into the heart of man the things which God has prepared for those who love Him (1 Corinthians 2:9).

So let each one give as he purposes in his heart, not grudgingly or of necessity, [*distress or need*]; for God loves a cheerful giver (2 Corinthians 9:7).

Speaking to one another in psalms and hymns and spiritual songs, singing and making melody in your heart to the Lord (Ephesians 5:19).

Now the purpose of the commandment is love from a pure [*clean and clear*] heart, from a good conscience, and from sincere faith (1Timothy 1:5).

Flee also youthful lusts [*desires*]; but pursue righteousness, faith, love, peace with those who call on the Lord out of a pure [*clean and clear*] heart (2 Timothy 2:22).

For the word of God is living and powerful, and sharper than any two-edged sword, piercing even to the division of soul and spirit, and of joints and marrow, and is a discerner of the thoughts and intents of the heart (Hebrews 4:12).

Let us draw near with a true heart in full assurance of faith [*conviction and truth*] having our hearts sprinkled from an evil conscience and our bodies washed with pure water (Hebrews 10:22).

Do not be carried about with various and strange doctrines, for it is good that the heart be established [*confirmed*] by grace, not with foods which have not profited those who have been occupied with them (Hebrews 13:9).

Since you have purified your souls in obeying the truth through the Spirit in sincere love of the brethren, love one another fervently with a pure heart (1 Peter 1:22).

Do not let your adornment be merely outward—arranging the hair, wearing of gold, or putting on fine apparel—rather let it be the hidden [*private, secret*] person of the heart, with the incorruptible beauty of a gentle and quiet spirit, which is very precious in the sight of God (1 Peter 3:3–4).

For if our heart condemns us [*finds fault*], God is greater than our heart, and knows all things. Beloved, if our heart does not condemn us [*finding fault*], we have confidence [*assurance and boldness*] toward God, and whatever we ask we receive from Him because we keep His commandments and do those things that are pleasing in His sight (1 John 3:20–22).

FOOTNOTES

[1] throughout section, additional words are written in brackets

[2] select words (For Ezra, his) were omitted and replaced by author

[3] select word (you) was omitted and replaced by author

[4] select words (his, his) were omitted and replaced by author

[5] select word (You) omitted and replaced by author

[6] select words (your, your, you, you) omitted and replaced by author

[7] select word (the) omitted and replaced by author

[8] select words (he, his, him, his) omitted and replaced by author

Prayer of Salvation

If you have never prayed the prayer of salvation, or if you are not sure whether you are saved, you can be sure right now.

Romans 10:9-10 says:

"...that if you confess with your mouth the Lord Jesus and believe in your heart that God has raised Him from the dead, you will be saved. For with the heart one believes unto righteousness, and with the mouth confession is made unto salvation."

Now repeat this prayer:

Father, I believe that you sent Jesus and He died on the Cross taking my sins upon Himself. I repent, right now, from all my sins, and I make a decision in my heart to turn away from anything that is not like Christ. Not only did Christ die for me, but I believe, Father, that You raised Him from the dead that I might be free; therefore, I receive Christ as my Savior and my Lord. Thank you Father God. I am now righteous because of the blood of Christ and His finished work on the Cross.

If you prayed this prayer, welcome to the family of God. It is important for you to tell someone that you have accepted Jesus as your personal Savior, and Lord over everything in your life. It is also important for you to find a local Bible believing and teaching church to attend on a weekly basis.

If you need assistance in finding a church, please contact me at this email address: wayoflifecc@yahoo.com.

Our website is www.wayoflifecc.com

You may contact Helen Canty Ministries directly for additional copies of *Eclipse of the Heart* as well as information on Helen Canty's speaking itinerary.

Canty Ministries
Email: cantyminitries@wayoflifecc.com
(248) 996-3152

Bibliography

AMG International, Inc. The Complete Word Study New Testament: AMG, 1992

AMG International, Inc. The Complete Word Study Old Testament: AMG, 1994

Bullinger, E. W. Number in Scripture: Kregel Publications, Grand Rapids

PC Study Bible, Seattle: Biblesoft, 1992-2002

Richards, James, Grace The Power To Change. New Kensington: Whitaker House, 1993

Strong, James, The New Strong's Exhaustive Concordance of the Bible: Nashville, Thomas Nelson, 1990

The Amplified Bible. Grand Rapids: Zondervan, 1987

About the Author

H ELEN C ANTY, along with her husband Fred, are pastors of *Way of Life Christian Church* in Canton, Michigan. Their vision to build people and help them reach their God given destiny has led Helen to write her first book, *Eclipse of the Heart.*

A believer for 27 years, Helen lived in a shroud of pain, unaware that her inward turmoil was a direct result of her own decisions. It wasn't until she realized God never intended for her to endure such agony that she made a conscious decision to stop living a co-dependent lifestyle. Exposing hidden pain was the beginning of healing, manifesting itself from the inside out. By the grace of God, she is not the same person she used to be.

It is Helen's sincere hope that *Eclipse of the Heart* will put her readers on the path to inward healing. Life is short. Don't delay taking steps necessary to walk in your God given destiny.

We do not get to push replay in life, nor will excuses allow us entrance into Heaven. Oh, to hear Him say when we meet Him face to face—*Well done, good and faithful servant!*

To order additional copies
of *Eclipse of the Heart*, or to find out about other books by
Helen Canty or Zoë Life Publishing, please visit our website
www.zoelifepub.com.

A bulk discount is available
when 12 or more books are purchased at one time.

Zoë Life Publishing
P.O. Box 871066
Canton, MI 48187
(877) 841-3400
outreach@zoelifepub.com

ZOË LIFE
PUBLISHING
WORDS TO LIVE BY